Lessons from the Good Old Days

Lessons from the
Good Old Days

Cliff Schimmels

VICTOR BOOKS

A DIVISION OF SCRIPTURE PRESS PUBLICATIONS INC.
USA CANADA ENGLAND

Copyediting: Carole Streeter; Barbara Williams
Cover Design: Scott Rattray
Cover Photo: FPG International

Library of Congress Cataloging-in-Publication Data

Schimmels, Cliff.

    Lessons from the good old days / Cliff Schimmels.

      p.   cm.

      1. Oklahoma—Social life and customs. 2. Values—Oklahoma.

    3. Schimmels, Cliff—Childhood and youth. I. Title.

    F700.S35 1994

  976.6—dc20   94-5076

                                                    CIP

---

1 2 3 4 5 6 7 8 9 10 Printing/Year 98 97 96 95 94

CONTENTS

CHAPTER ONE
The Good Old Days

"DO YOU REMEMBER the good old days when we used to go to the pond and feed the ducks?" Alyssa asked me one day last summer, and on her cue I remembered. I took my mind way back into a distant past when life was simpler and purer and we were both younger, and I remembered with joy those endless summer days when we spent long idle afternoons staring into the water and throwing bread crumbs to the ducks. It was a pleasant experience for me, this activity of remembering, and I appreciated Alyssa's challenge to relive it.

Of course, Alyssa is my six-year-old granddaughter, and her good old days were two years ago when she was four. But that's all right.

That's what this book is about—a journey back into the good old days, regardless of how long ago they were.

"What is this?" you ask rather impatiently. "A nostalgic romp somewhere between rose-colored romanticism and bad memory?" If that is what the book is, let it be.

Someone once said that those who don't learn their history are condemned to repeat it. I don't know whether that is a threat or a promise, but at least it's an axiom worth noting. To face the present, and also what lies ahead in that dreaded far-off time six years from now in the twenty-first century, we need to pause occasionally and take a look at our history.

Since this book is about life during my boyhood and young adulthood, it focuses on the decades of the forties, the fifties, and the sixties. And that's important because most of us know far more about the Civil War than we do about the fifties. When we were students in history class, the semester always ended somewhere during World War I. Just consider this book as a starting place from where your last history class left off.

Not long ago, I heard a speaker say that we are now living in the post-modern age. I'm not sure I know what that means; but if it is more than one of those catchy buzzwords we use to keep from communicating with each other, then surely it means that we've endured a transition somctime during our lifetime. That makes it rather valuable for us to study those years we call the good old days, to see how we moved beyond modernity to whatever comes next.

Instead of looking at characters in full-dress uniforms as most history books do, this book takes a look at that segment of society that didn't even own full-dress uniforms, much less pose in them. This book is about common people living common lives doing common things, and that's the real story of history.

But this book is not really meant to be a history book. Instead it is designed to be a book about parenting. But even in that role, it's a little different. I have now reached that age when I make plans by retrospect. I've discovered that we're all products of our own personal history. In other words, we are cumulative creatures. Through our lives we have accumulated a variety of experiences and emotions and perspectives, and all of those loom large in what we do today.

Now that I've gotten to the place in life where the pace has slowed a bit and the battle doesn't rage so urgently, I've had time to assess my life, and I've concluded that my parents knew quite a lot about the science of parenting. Without boasting too much about the way I turned out, just let me say that they did a fair job in many respects.

I once heard James Dobson say, "We're so busy giving our children what we never had that we forget to give them what we did have." That's what this journey to the good old days is about—what our parents did give us.

Most books on parenting talk about the intentional acts. They give us checklists of parenting rules, and we can tick off those items we get right on purpose and those we don't. That's good. I like those tick-off check-lists, particularly on days when my batting average is up; on days when I'm going to feel a little guilty about those rules, I avoid the checklists.

But have you ever noticed that many of the memories you have about the good times and the good lessons you had with your parents were in those unintentional moments when neither party stopped to realize, "Wow, this is an eternal learning experience we're having here!" Our parents didn't mean to be good teachers. They just were, and to think that they did it all by accident!

I offer this observation as encouragement. Maybe parenting isn't as big a mystery as we make it out to be. I do know that parenting isn't the exact science some of the checklist books imply. Maybe good parenting is still what it was when we were the kids and our parents were in charge. Maybe it's just a matter of hanging around, providing a few experiences, and then responding to them. Maybe the best education on the science of parenting that we can get is to spend a few evenings remembering some of those times and reassuring ourselves that we are indeed giving similar experiences to our children. That's what this book is about.

Now, don't waste too much time searching this book for those earthshaking moments of immortal history written in red on worldwide calendars and chronicles. If we're not careful, we can delude ourselves into thinking that growing up is hopping from hill to hill, never taking time to notice the valleys in between. But life is more about the valleys than the hills. In my advanced years, I've sort of lost memory of the hills, but I remember the ordinary days, a smile, a casual word, a pat on the back; the day Dad did just a little extra for me and forgot as soon as he had done it; the day Mom took a moment to doctor a hurt that wasn't all that hurt, but needed emotional attention instead. These are the good old days that keep creeping back into my conscious being and dictating attitudes and emotions that I know are proper half a century later.

I hear people say that *life* was simpler back in the good old days. I don't know whether that's true, but probably *we* were simpler, and in our simplicity we drank deeply from the clear springs of everyday living. And those sips and gulps from our experiences still nourish us. We learned then, and we're learning still.

There is, however, a certain limitation in learning from this approach. My background is mine. I write from the perspective of a farm boy growing up in western Oklahoma, mostly during the fifties. If your good old days are not the same as mine in place or time, play the game with me anyway. Although the setting may be specific, the thesis is universal. If you had parents who loved you and wanted you to get it right in life, you surely have some spot in your personal chronicle that you can hook a memory to.

For full therapeutic value, I would like to prescribe this book to you in proper doses. If you are about my age, you are too old to be drinking much warm milk at bedtime, so take this book instead. Don't read it all in one sitting. Instead, put it by your bedside and take one dose nightly. You may find that my story isn't all that appropriate and you have a better one to tell. That won't hurt my feelings. Start thinking about your better story from your good old days, get comfortable and pleasant in your memory, and drop off to sleep that way. You'll be a more charming person when you awake tomorrow. That will make you a better parent, and your children will profit from my labors. That's what this book is about.

Chapter Two

Filling Stations

IN THE GOOD old days, grocery stores did not sell gasoline. Filling stations sold gasoline, and they did not sell groceries, except for pop. Pop was, in fact, a necessary item at filling stations because it came in sturdy wooden cases, and filling stations operated on those pop cases. They served many purposes. Pop cases were used as car blocks when it came time to change the tires or put on a new set of brakes. Pop cases stacked on top of each other worked as stepladders when the filling station man needed to climb to the top of the store to get a new inner tube. But the most important function of pop cases was as furniture. That's where the community Spit and Whittle Club sat during their daily meetings, which were always held at the filling stations.

Filling stations also sold candy, but not very much; their candy was always stale and full of weevils, because it had been displayed in those big glass cases for months and months.

In the good old days, you did not pump gasoline into your car. The filling station man pumped the gas, and most of us didn't even know how to unlock the mystery of making a gas pump work. That was the untold secret of the filling station man. You could always identify the filling station man by the way he dressed. You would never mistake him for the banker or even for the members of the Spit and Whittle Club who spent hours every day sitting on those upturned pop cases. The Beau Brummels of the filling station men wore leather bow ties; but the distinguishing characteristic of all of them, from the best dressed to the shabbiest, was that red grease rag hanging from a pocket. My older sister and I once had an argument about whether the filling station man even wore the grease rag to bed at night. She didn't see much need of it, but I still thought that a habit was a habit and couldn't be broken on the strength of logic alone.

The filling station man pumped the gasoline into your car, but he did more than that. He washed the windshield, lifted the hood to check the oil, felt the radiator to see if it was running cool enough, and glanced at all four tires just to make sure you weren't about to have a flat. If he was really efficient, he carried a little whisk broom which he used to sweep around your feet. This was service, and some filling stations were so proud of it that they even bragged by putting the word into their name and calling themselves "Service Stations."

But at the filling station, you got more than gasoline and service. You also got the news. This was one of the great timesaving features of the good old days. You didn't have to stay up past eleven every night to get the local news.

In the filling station edition of the news, the weather report always came first. Usually the weather report was incorporated into the greeting. As the filling station man approached your car and you were rolling down the window to speak to him, his first words were, "Hot enough for you!" His utterance was not a question, but an objective report disguised in the language of a question. He meant to tell you that it was hot enough for you. "No hope for rain today. Maybe tomorrow, if the wind shifts to the south." And there was the weather report in about ten seconds — complete, up-to-date and just as reliable as all that stuff that comes with the TV charts and arrows and computer cloud movements.

This was the opening of the news report. The rest of the local news came in thirty-second bites as the filling station man moved around your car performing his various service functions. Actually these thirty-second bites were the forerunners to today's television report, but there was one major difference. The filling station newscast was interactive, demanding responses from you at the appropriate moments.

"Too bad about old Adolph," the filling station man would say with genuine concern, as he dragged a wet chamois across your windshield.

"Oh," you would say with astonishment, fulfilling your responsibility with enthusiasm. "I hadn't heard."

"Oh, yeah," the filling station man would continue, with full assurance that you had not changed channels. "Fell off his barn. Broke his leg in two places. Ambulance had to come out and get him. Came by here with all those lights blinking and sirens wailing. They're fixing to put a pin in his leg. Just wire him back together. That's the way they do things nowadays. But I guess it won't bother old George none, will it?''

In the language of TV, that last sentence is what is known as a segue. Without any new camera angles or any rolling pictures, this was the filling station version of a transition. The old bite was finished and the new one was about to begin. But it was your responsibility to indicate that you were still tuned in, so you had to ask at that moment, "Why not? Where's George?"

"Went to California." The filling station man would begin the second byte. "Took the whole family. They're going to be gone for two whole weeks. I'll bet they'll have stories to tell when they get home." In the good old days, a two-week vacation was indeed special enough to justify a place in the local news report, particularly a vacation to somewhere as far off and exotic as California.

Thus, the news report continued as the filling station man worked his way around your car and you picked up service plus.

Filling station men often had professionally appropriate names such as Bus or Truck or Otto. These were the names we knew them by, and everybody in the community could identify them by those names because they were semifamous. But when we quoted them later to our neighbors, we called them by another name. In reference, we always called them Somebody.

"Somebody told me that Adolph broke his leg," we would say, and our audience could immediately deduce that we had a full tank of gasoline and a clean windshield.

Filling station men were usually capable in all areas of automobile service, but each had a specialty. One would be so skillful at cleaning windshields that his talent would go beyond skill, and he could actually be considered an artist. He would study windshields, cleaners, and cloths until he knew just the right combination for the specific challenge before him, and he took pride in his accomplishment. Some even would advertise it. "Cleanest windshield in town," the handwritten sign by the side of the road would announce.

Not long ago I took a group of college students on a trip, and one young lady appointed herself as the windshield cleaner every time we stopped at those do-it-yourself grocery store gas pumps. She approached her task with a sense of artistic accomplishment reminiscent of the good old days, and I got misty-eyed just thinking about it.

My personal favorite among the automobile service artists was the man who was talented at checking the oil. Perhaps I appreciated him because I am rather clumsy at handling that flimsy stick, and my hand and eye coordination still requires several jabs to get the thing where it is supposed to be. But Bus was an artist. Regardless of how long that dipstick was and where the automobile manufacturer had tried to hide it amidst all those other gadgets and do bobs, Bus could whip that thing out, wipe it clean with one continuous motion, and jab it back with action almost too fast for the naked eye to see. It was a thing of beauty just to watch him check the oil. Some days when he didn't have many customers and there were people at the Spit and Whittle meeting he was trying to impress, Bus would even twirl the thing or fake a little fencing action as if it were a rapier blade. In those days, buying gasoline always came with some entertainment feature.

Of course the old-timers who bought gasoline before there were electric pumps will have other kinds of service favorites. In those really olden days, the filling station man who had some flair for pumping that five-gallon glass bowl full before he started the gas flow into your car was very talented. In those days we bought gasoline by the gallon because that kept the bowl accurate, and the filling station man would compute what we owed by multiplying our gallons by the appropriate price. I remember my first trip to a large city: Wichita, Kansas. One of my biggest thrills was that my cousin bought gasoline by the dollar amount instead of by the gallon. I knew then that we were living in the truly post-modern age.

But in addition to all that gasoline, service, and news, filling stations served another function in our lives. They gave us a sense of belonging. Almost as much as we belonged to a church or a service organization, we belonged to the filling station and to the man who ran it. We paid our dues, we had a sense of membership, and we definitely felt a sense of loyalty. On rare occasions, some upstart down the road would sell gasoline at a bargain price, and we would sneak off and fill our tank.

But we always felt guilty about it. For the whole next week when we would drive by Bus', he would wave really big, and we would be ashamed for what we had done. We couldn't wait until we had used up at least half a tank so we could go back to Bus for gasoline, service, news, and conscience clearing.

As I get older and hopefully a little wiser, I have come to realize that this sense of belonging is one of the basic human needs. We all need to belong to something. We see evidence of this every day. We read about groups of seemingly intelligent people who follow some leader off into isolation and make a suicide pact, and we are amazed. We wonder why innocent children living in the heart of the city join gangs and pay a horrible price for their membership. But in the old days, I belonged to the gang that bought gasoline from Bus. It was more than service. It was an identity. At parties where we were often surrounded by strangers, those of us who shopped at Bus' would gravitate toward each other and spend the evening talking about Adolph's broken leg or George's California vacation. We held something in common. We belonged to Bus and we belonged to each other.

In these current times, discount prices and convenience have changed all that. We don't belong to retailers anymore. We buy where we can get the bargains; we run all over town trying to find them, and we aren't ashamed. In fact, I have even seen people dressed in the uniform of one discount store shopping in another. Loyalty and belonging aren't factors in our shopping habits, but we still have the need. Just as blessings always carry obligations, so convenience always entails some hardship, and we must learn to pay the price.

Buying gasoline from Bus was only a minor part of my life in the good old days, but it was still integral; and now that I've lost it, I have to find a wholesome substitute. Thanks to Bus, I at least know what I'm looking for.

Chapter Three

The Potato Bug Industry

BEFORE MCDONALD'S, WE had potato bugs. I read somewhere that one out of every eight workers presently working in the United States had a first job with McDonald's. Isn't that amazing? When you think of all the other fast-food places throughout the country, it staggers the mind to try to compute what percentage of American workers enter the labor force through the hamburger industry.

In the good old days, we didn't have fast-food shops. We had hamburger joints, but they weren't manned by neophyte adolescents. They were staffed by big burly guys named Ralph who had tattooed mothers glaring out from beneath their sleeves.

Our entry into the labor force was through the potato bug industry, and we managed to get in at a much earlier age than today's kids in their smart uniforms. Usually, our first real employment was quite unintentional. One day we would be listening to the radio and would hear of some magic item for sale for just one cornflakes box top and twenty-five cents. To fully comprehend this lure, you have to understand the power of a child's imagination. That magic item might have been a decoder ring that would actually interpret secret messages and which, as we all remember from the cold war, was a necessity in every home. That magic item might have been a special pen with a flashlight built right into it so that you could write secret messages in the dark. Or that magic item might have been a remarkable rope which was so rigged that you could twirl it like a real cowboy and impress all your friends.

Regardless of the whim of your imagination at the particular moment you heard the radio ad, you knew that you *had* to own the thing. Ownership of that one item was the only thing that stood between you and true happiness.

Getting the first half of the required purchase price was no problem. You could just go in and tear the top off the cornflakes box. If anyone complained, you could eat cornflakes for supper just to use up the remainder before it got stale or weevils. But getting the quarter was another kind of obstacle. At that point, you needed support for the item of your imagination. Now I never fully understood why mothers were so passive at this point. Usually, mothers, having once been children themselves, had at least some respect for the imagination, and they should have known how important that magic item was and how urgent the whole matter was. Who knows — maybe spies were trying to contact us even now, and we wouldn't know it because we did not have a decoder ring. But for all their other charming qualities, mothers were usually passive about the magic item on the radio. Later when I became a parent, I realized the reason. They had once been suckered on the magic item lure, and they knew the disappointment we were about to let ourselves in for. But mothers, understanding that some suffering is necessary for true learning, never said no. Instead they took that opportunity to put us into the work force.

"I'm sorry, but if you want a quarter, you'll just have to work for it," Mother would say with a serious, slave-driver tone in her voice and a little grin on her face.

"What do I have to do?" I would ask, hoping that my assignment might involve some risk connected to my need for the magic item.

"Well, somebody needs to go out to the garden and pick bugs off the potato plants," Mother would answer.

Depressed by the earthy nature of the assignment, I would ask, "How much does it pay?" In the good old days, we weren't as sophisticated as today's children. We didn't ask about retirement benefits, insurance packages, or severance pay guarantees. We just asked about basic salary.

"I'll pay a penny per bug," Mother would answer. It is important to point out here that the potato bug industry is completely immune to economic instability, inflation, or depression. Ever since I can remember, the going rate for picking potato bugs has been a penny a bug—never more, never less.

With the salary agreed, we got ourselves a bucket and went to work. Contrary to what you might be thinking, the potato bug industry was not as one-dimensional as it may sound. There were so many ways to go about it that picking potato bugs allowed us the freedom to define not only our work habits but even our personalities.

There were many different kinds of workers in the field. First, there were the daintyites. These were usually girls, but sometimes cousins who were visiting from the city, who would go along picking bugs with the tips of their fingers, and then saying "OOOOH" with each pick. Regardless of where you were in the potato patch, you could always tell their success because you could count the number of OOOOHs. But they weren't finished by just going "OOOH." They still had the challenge of depositing the bug in the bucket, and that always required skill that only the daintyites had. Ever so gently, they would find a place for the bug amidst all the other bugs so that they wouldn't disturb the ecosystem of the bucket when they dropped it.

Other kinds of workers in the industry were the top-leaf sprites. These people were in a hurry. Their only objective was to get the bucket full, and they didn't care all that much about reducing the population of bugs in any one location. They ran through the patch helter-skelter. Never stooping, never searching through the leaves for the really vicious monsters, these workers just grabbed the bugs that were out sunning themselves on the top leaves; and with the same velocity that they ran through the field, they would run home for a count.

The other kind of worker in the potato bug industry was the grubber. I was a grubber. We took our job seriously. We were out to get the bugs, all the bugs, and we went after them with aggressiveness, regardless of where they might be hiding. We got down on our hands and knees and searched through the dirt. Of course, sometimes we did mistake a little clod for a potato bug and deposited that in the bucket too. After all, according to Ben Franklin, "A penny is a penny," or something like that.

But the major feature of our work is that we got dirty. When we were finished, we had done a day's work, and we had something to show for it — dirty clothes.

When it was all over and we had grown either tired or rich, we went in and settled up with our mother. After we had earned our quarter, by the sweat of our brow and the dirt under our fingernails, something else happened to us. Somehow that magic item just didn't have the lure that it had when we first thought of it. Now that we had the quarter, we could think of several more sensible ways to spend the money. And that was the magic of the potato bug industry. Earning our own money took the romance out of the magic.

I really don't want to make light of this point. Through our efforts in the potato patch, we learned that there is a direct relationship between work and being able to buy something, and that is a good lesson to learn. But there is a deeper lesson here as well. Work is a satisfying activity. When we work, we feel good about ourselves. When we don't work, we have to fill that need in our life with some other means. And that's the lure of the magic items advertised on the radio.

I've heard the present crop of young people accused

of being lazy, worthless, spoiled spendthrifts. But I don't agree. They have the same needs as we did when we were their age. To fill that need, they have the same two choices we had—buy a decoder ring or pick bugs off the potato vines.

CHAPTER FOUR

The Day the Preacher Came to Dinner

WHEN I WAS small, our preacher was big. Although he didn't have that typical broad and husky preacher build, he was tall. He had a long body and a long face, and he wore his hair combed straight back, giving him the appearance of having an endless head. And when he stepped up to the pulpit, he grew another three feet. He had a deep voice that bellowed out and shook the room and the parishioners' insides.

The preacher's wife was a frail little woman who looked frightened by it all. I didn't blame her. I was frightened too. I don't recall many of the preacher's sermons from those days, but I do remember that I spent most of my time in church being frightened. For one thing, when the preacher talked to God in his prayers, he spoke in a foreign language with words I didn't know, such as Thou and Thine and peerless. Since I didn't know that language, I was afraid to talk to God in my common everyday boy words, so I avoided prayer as often as I could.

The preacher's messages were frightening too. I think

that was by design, and with me he achieved full effect. I remember one particularly, because he said it almost every Sunday. He would get a grave look on his face, fluff his hair up even taller, stretch his arm out in full extension pointing that one finger at every one of us at the same time, and then he would ask, "What would you do if Jesus came to your house for dinner today?" And I shuddered at the thought of the impending judgment and wrath.

Jesus never came, but the preacher did. One Friday evening as we were just finishing supper, Mom said, "I think what this family needs is to have the preacher over for Sunday dinner." Dad agreed, and the plan was in place. But in my boyish naiveté, I made an error in calculation. I thought the preacher would come the next Sunday and we would be done with it. Not so. Mom asked him three weeks in advance. I made another error in calculation. When she set the date, I thought she had to ask three weeks in advance so that the preacher could prepare. Not so. She gave a three-week notice so that we could prepare. And we spent the whole three weeks preparing for the day that the preacher would come to dinner.

Not long ago I spoke in a church one Sunday morning. When one of the families came and asked if I could have Sunday dinner with them, I got out my calendar to check what I had to do in three weeks. But they assured me that they meant right now, and so I went with them. They bought a bucket of chicken, and the whole ordeal of having the preacher for dinner was over in a wink. My, how times have changed!

We prepared for three solid weeks. First, we cleaned the house. We didn't just clean the house. WE CLEANED THE HOUSE! We didn't just gather up the old newspapers and the dirty socks lying around. We mopped, we dusted, we washed the windows and scrubbed down the walls. Mom even made us kids clean our own rooms, and I never understood the reason for that. It just seemed to me that we could throw the junk into our rooms and close the doors and just make sure the preacher didn't go in. But she wouldn't accept that, so we had to clean. I suspected that the preacher had some power like Superman and could see through closed doors.

To finish off our cleaning madness, we washed all the good china, and then we polished the wedding silver. Let me explain. At our house, we had a mystery box—a big beautiful mahogany box which sat in a prominent place in the middle of our dining room. Inside that box was the wedding silver. We knew that mostly by legend instead of direct observation, because we wouldn't dare to peek inside. This was the family's most prized possession, more dear even than the children, particularly when you considered us as individuals. Somebody had given my parents the silverware as a wedding gift when they were married, but it was too priceless to use. I always suspected it was too holy to use for something as common as eating. During all my years of living in that household, we used the wedding silverware once—the day the preacher came.

The second part of the preacher-day preparation was

choosing the proper chicken. The very day she had is-
sued the invitation, Mom went out and picked a young
rooster for the distinctive honor of entering the ministry.
For three weeks, we fed that chicken a little extra and
treated him with kindness in respect for the sacrifice he
was destined to make for the spreading of the Good
News.

The really tough part of the preparation was the inten-
sive manner training. We had to go through this every
meal for three weeks, and it wasn't easy. For one thing,
we had to rearrange the seating chart. Through the
years, I've noticed that you can mess with many traditions without causing serious psychological damage. I've
known ministers who have actually changed the order of
Sunday service and lived to tell about it. I've seen baby
girls dressed in blue. But the one tradition that you don't
want to mess with is the family seating arrangement
around the table. That one is sacred . . . until the preacher comes. The preacher was to sit in Daddy's chair and
his wife was to sit next to him in my older brother's spot.
Well, of course, that just brought chaos to the entire
process. The only person who was permitted to keep her
cherished spot was Mom. I don't mean to overstate it,
but this new arrangement didn't come easy. We had to
rehearse it several times before we got it right. It also
complicated the passing scheme. We were to pass everything to the preacher first so that all dishes began with
him. Of course, that meant that he got to pick his piece
of chicken from the top. I still don't know which one he
picked, but by the time the plate came all the way down

to me, I got the neck.

The big day arrived. The preacher and his wife came to our house for Sunday dinner, but I was so nervous and uptight about it all that I don't really remember much about what actually happened, except that I ate the chicken neck. But this visit was a major event—maybe the major event in the history of the Schimmels' family. Somehow our whole home took on a special holy aura. We had performed a significant spiritual duty, and we knew it. We had fed the preacher, and we bragged about it. For years to come, we would casually drop it into conversation. Five years later, I heard Mom say to the lady next door, "Well, the preacher was over at our house for dinner, and he told me . . ."

During the years since then, I've read the Bible a little myself and I've visited around a bit, and I've come to a rather refreshing conclusion. If I had a choice, I would rather have Jesus for dinner than the preacher. I don't believe that it would be nearly as frightening and wouldn't require nearly as much preparation. In fact, Jesus fussed at one lady who was going through too much bustle in preparation for His coming to dinner. "Forget the cleaning," He said. "Let's just sit around and talk to each other for now. You can clean house after I leave."

I also think that Jesus would stick around and help wash dishes. That preacher sure didn't. In fact, it took us almost as long to clean up after he ate as it did to prepare beforehand, especially when we had to repolish the wedding silverware before we put it back into storage.

On the other hand, Jesus had a record of doing little things to help, like making a fire and cooking breakfast for the disciples who were hungry from fishing all night. I think the preacher was just trying to scare us. I believe having Jesus over for dinner would be a very pleasant experience; and to be honest, I'm looking forward to it.

CHAPTER FIVE

Why Car Doors Don't Open from the Front

EVERYBODY HAS HIS or her own idea of what a classic car is. What gets your vote? A 1955 Thunderbird? A 1957 Chevy? A 1952 Desoto?

My choice of the all-time most beautiful car ever made, the true classic, the car above all cars, is the 1948 Plymouth. The reason that car is so special to me is that it was the first new car we ever bought. We had managed to live through the war years driving junkers and clunkers, and when the war ended and the economy improved, we had some inkling that maybe our fate was about to change. But Dad still took us by surprise one evening when he came motoring up the drive in a brand-new, beige, four-door 1948 Plymouth. I shall never forget the look on his face when he got out amidst our stares of disbelief and wonder. He was pleased that he had surprised us, but he was also pleased that he could provide us with something that we obviously appreciated so much.

That Plymouth was not just the most beautiful car I had ever seen. It was the most beautiful machine of any kind I had ever seen, and it was running a close contest with being the most beautiful object of creation I had ever seen. At that particular time, I was not mature enough to be a connoisseur of the beauty of the human female so I was caught between admiring the sky on a starry fall night or a certain cow I thought had come as close to perfect as anything could be.

But that car was truly beautiful. Not being old enough to drive, I would just go out and sit in the car by the hour. I wasn't really wasting time. In addition to being in awe of such beauty, I also dreamed and made plans and imagined that I was traveling to far-off and exotic places amidst the stares of those along the road who had never seen a car as beautiful as ours. All that imagining had an educational value as well. I would take the road atlas with me and study the routes to the places I would visit — places like Carlsbad Caverns, Yosemite National Park, the Smoky Mountains, and, yes, even Dodge City. Not only did I dream but I learned geography too, and I fell in love with the U.S. and with traveling while sitting in that motionless car.

Our 1948 Plymouth had some interesting features. The gearshift was on the steering column instead of in the middle of the floor, like all the other cars I had seen before. This may not seem like a major advancement in the line of great inventions in the history of the world to anyone who is not a middle child. But we middle children can attest to the true genius of that major technological breakthrough. In those days, middle children had to sit in the middle of the front seat, straddling the gearshift. Just sitting there straddle-legged was wearisome enough by itself, but it took on a special kind of torture in hill country or on dirt roads where Daddy had to shift a lot. He was always bumping me and hitting me or growling at me, as if it were my fault that he couldn't shift gracefully.

That gearshift on the column in the Plymouth eliminated all that bumping and hitting and growling, and surely eliminated some serious pyschological distress that had once plagued middle children everywhere. Besides that, when we boys got older and dated in that car, that steering column arrangement allowed for our girlfriends to sit closer.

Another feature of that 1948 Plymouth was that the rear doors opened from the front. I'm not sure I know any utilitarian reason for this. Perhaps it is something of a more natural movement for the body in the backseat to lurch forward a bit to exit the automobile. Perhaps this getting up and out at the same time made sense to the engineers who designed the doors.

Regardless of the utilitarian reason, there was a fashionable reason for the doors to open from the front. That is the way the doors worked on the bigger and fancier automobiles. We learned that tidbit of elegance at the movies on Saturday afternoons. Before the main feature and even before the cliff-hanging serial each Saturday, the weekly edition of Movie Time News always showed at least one shot of the Hollywood stars or high-powered government officials or other members of the rich and famous set attending a major event. They would arrive in their big limos and make a grand exit into the midst of their admiring fans. Those limousine doors always opened from the front, and the Enviable Ones would manage to stand right there at the door and wave to all of us commoners while they were still mostly in the car. It was so romantic. Somehow they were reaching out to be a part of us, yet they were still halfway protected by the elegance and security of their lavish automobile.

It was a scene to put yourself into in your imagining moments — when you received the Nobel Prize, right after you had pitched the winning game of the World Series, when you were winning an award for being the greatest singing cowboy in the world. There I would be, getting out of my limo and waving to my admirers all in one movement. I even had some concrete help for my dreaming. We owned a 1948 Plymouth with the doors opening from the front, and I could practice.

One day while I was still in the middle of feeling good about that engineering feat and my future, I learned why that arrangement might not have been one of the best features on the car. My older brother and I were driving our little sister somewhere. She was about five years old at the time, and it seemed as if we were always driving her someplace. My brother was driving and I was riding shotgun, another phrase left over from the good old days. Sandy was in the backseat, but she was standing up, leaning across to the front to make conversation. It was a nice arrangement and a rather common one for us, for a couple of reasons. For one thing, we didn't want her riding in the front seat, and she liked making conversation.

I have forgotten what the conversation was about, but I remember that there was a period of silence. Since that was a rather rare occurrence when Sandy was in the backseat, my brother and I turned around to see if there might be a problem. That's when we discovered the defect with doors that opened elegantly from the front. Sandy had inadvertently put her foot on the handle of the right door. The door swung open with the force of wind blowing at forty miles per hour, and Sandy, obedient to natural force, abandoned the automobile. When we spotted her, she was in the drainage ditch about one hundred yards behind us, waving frantically and still making conversation. At that point I decided that utility was the better part of elegance, and that car doors should not open from the front.

I learned a couple of worthwhile lessons from that 1948 Plymouth. In my memory, it remains to this day a fine automobile, full of comfort, beauty, and elegance. I'm not alone in all that kind of remembering. Those of us who spend our time reliving the good old days frequently focus on the automobile world. We sigh for what we have lost, shake our heads sorrowfully in disbelief and say, "Well, they just don't make them like they used to." That's the creed, the catechism. Any person past forty is supposed to make that statement almost daily. But the truth is that in some ways, we're probably rather happy that they don't make them like they did in the good old days. In the good old days, we got ten thousand miles on a set of tires. About every thirty thousand miles we had to take the machine in to get the valves ground.

And the doors opened from the front. The lesson I learned from the 1948 Plymouth is that we learn from our mistakes. With enough Sandys deposited in enough ditches around the country, automobile manufacturers learned that a car's doors should not open from the front, and they just took one more worry out of being a parent. Despite our selective remembering, those classic automobiles had some faults. They were not as perfect as we remember them to be.

The other thing I learned from that incident with the Plymouth was that there were certain events we never shared with our parents. All three of us kept it a secret. At the time, we thought that we were doing ourselves a favor. We were a little afraid that if we told them, they might not let us drive again. But through the years, as I have watched my own children grow up, I have come to realize that we were doing our parents a favor too. There are some things that the parents really don't need to know about until later, when distance has erased the panic of possible danger.

Now that my children are all grown and living productive, worthwhile lives as they raise their own children, I enjoy getting together with them and just sitting and listening to their conversations about their own growing days. Every time, I learn about some other event in the past that they forgot to tell me . . . the time they almost had a wreck, or when they almost drowned playing in an off-limits farm pond. If I had known every detail with all the possible traps and dangers at the time they happened, I would have either become totally gray, a raving lunatic, or one of those tyrannical parents who locks his children away in a closet, far removed from the dangers of an outside world. Praise God that my children were bright enough to spare me all the vivid details at the time.

But now as they relate the stories from the perspective of a distant past and they laugh about their own follies and near misses, I learn the true lesson that I might not have seen so clearly in those days. We don't raise them alone. Despite all our efforts to give them the best we have and to protect them from every possible danger, we simply can't keep them from all those near misses. Our only hope is to trust the One who holds them in the palm of His hand and counts the hairs on their heads, even on the day they gave each other a haircut.

CHAPTER SIX

Ice Cream on a Sunday Afternoon

FROM MY TRAVELS to various spots in the world, I have discovered one universal truth about childrearing. Every young person in every geographical region in the whole world has grown weary of hearing his parents tell stories about how rough life was in the old days. I don't do that. I don't stand around and bore my children with those exaggerated tales of my walking three miles to school each day—which I did, through snow and rain and dirt storms, I could add. I don't go for the sympathy act by telling them that we had to work all summer, slaving in the cotton patch under a blazing hot sun just to get one pair of shoes. For one thing, I doubt that they would believe it, particularly when I add that we three children shared that one pair of shoes among us.

But the one story of hardship which I think I have a right to tell, and which I think they should be obligated to hear over and over, is the story of ice cream. How fortunate children are these days because they don't have to make the supreme sacrifice for ice cream.

Of course, we had ice cream when I was a child. Let

me answer that question before it is asked. How old do you think I am? But we just didn't run around the corner and pick up a carton. We had to suffer for our ice cream, and suffering is good for us. It builds character and appetite.

It would always occur on a Sunday afternoon. We would have company, and the old folks would all be sitting around telling stories about how rough life was when they were children and how we modern brats didn't appreciate anything. As I remember it now, I think I would grow weary of hearing the stories and would doze off a bit. Then someone would say, "Wouldn't a dish of ice cream hit the spot about now?" and everyone would perk up and acknowledge approval with nods, smiles, and hearty "amens."

At this point, life turned to temporary misery for me. My dad would look at me and say as nonchalantly as if he were giving a weather report, "Clifford, run out and get a cow in and milk her so we can have some ice cream." I must add that historical record is a bit controversial here. My records indicate that he always gave me the assignment. Other records, those lodged in the deepest memories of my brother and sisters, report that they too sometimes got the assignment. Since I can't document that, I must maintain my original position. I had to go milk a cow.

In order for you to get the full impact of that duty, you must understand something about cows. They have eating habits different from humans. They don't sit down at the table, gobble till their bellies are full, and then go off to spend the rest of the afternoon wishing they hadn't eaten so much at one sitting. Instead, they use more of a chat and nibble approach. They nibble a bit, stand around and chat with their neighbors, and then nibble a bit more. That's the way they spend most of the day—chatting and nibbling. That's why cows are more content than humans. They have smarter eating habits.

Cows also time their chatting and nibbling so that they can finish both activities about six o'clock in the afternoon. That is the natural pattern for cows. To interrupt that pattern is to commit a serious breech of animal etiquette. In other words, to round up a cow at three o'clock and encourage her to walk a mile back to the milking barn is a disruption of the most basic and fundamental natural law. Suffice it to say that the cow did not want to go with me, even after I had said "Shoo" and "Scat" and "Skidaddle" and some other words our Sunday School teachers had asked us not to say.

After resorting to other forms of persuasion, some of which bordered on violence, I would finally get the cow back to the barn. Now it's time for another lesson about cows. Euphemisms are a cruel form of speech. They cover up the true spirit of the event by glossing it over with fancy words. One of the cruelest euphemisms in the English language pertains to cows. Everyone talks as if cows *give* milk. "How much milk does your cow give?" they ask.

Let me correct the erroneous thinking implied by that vicious and inaccurate euphemism. Cows do not *give* milk. Cows *have* milk, but if you want it, you have to *take* it away from them. They have no intention of letting you have it. If you want it, you have to engage in a contest just short of mortal battle. There is a logical reason for this. If you have ever seen a cow milked, you must admit that it is a rather undignified occasion for both the cow and the person doing the milking.

At six o'clock cows are content from having completed their day by doing what they set out to do, so they put up only mild resistance to milking. But at three o'clock, the cow I had driven up, not understanding anything about the human craving for ice cream, was in a bad mood and was wholly determined that I should not have any milk. But I was more determined and always succeeded to get at least enough for us to have ice cream.

Battered, bruised, and hoping there were no broken bones, I would bring in my bucket of milk. My mother would mix it with some other ingredients including ice cream powder, boil it a minute or two, and pour it into the freezer where it would be turned into a Sunday afternoon delicacy.

As we took the first refreshing bites, everyone would turn to my mother and exclaim with deepest appreciation, "Oh, this is so good. You have just worked a miracle."

And all the time I would sit there, licking my spoon, nursing my wounds, and thinking to myself, "What about the guy who milked the cow? Why doesn't he get any credit for this?"

One day Jesus went to a party. It was a wedding, actually. In the course of the merriment, they ran out of wine, which seemed to be a serious predicament at weddings in those days. But Mary was there and she sprang into action and faith. She told people to do what her Son said. After a word of protest, Jesus instructed the servants to fill the water jars. Jesus then turned the water into wine which was so rich and good that even the head wine expert was amazed. That was a great miracle indeed and one with so many deep theological lessons that I won't even attempt to discuss why Mary believed or why Jesus protested or even why He decided to break into His ministry of miracles at a wedding. But I do want to point out some people who get overlooked in this story. What about those servants who filled the water jars? Let's not forget them and the role they played in this miracle.

Of course, if Jesus had wanted to, He could have made the wine out of nothing. Incidentally, He had done that once before at the beginning of it all, so He had precedent.

However, this time Jesus had the servants fill the water jars, and then He turned the water into wine. In fact, this became the pattern for Jesus' ministry. Notice how often in performing a miracle Jesus would require the services of an obedient servant. I find this both encouraging and challenging. Sometimes we sit around and brood that Jesus isn't in the miracle business anymore, but maybe He is. Maybe He just needs some obedient servant to help Him.

Not long ago my wife, Mary, and I had a misunderstanding about something that seemed more important then than it does now. Miraculously, Jesus calmed the storm. Of course, I had to wash the dishes, but Jesus calmed the storm.

Last summer some students from the college where I teach traveled to the Ukraine and told a young doctor the good news of eternity. The man believed and the next day he was killed in an automobile accident. Miraculously, Jesus had snatched him out of a burning pit.

The question isn't really whether Jesus is capable of performing miracles. We know that He is. Instead, the question is whether we're willing to help Him.

The question was never whether ice cream was a possibility. Instead, the question was whether I was willing to milk a cow.

Chapter Seven

Box Suppers

ONCE UPON A time when the world was young, there were no shopping malls. That great absence in civilization worked hardships upon all people. Adults had to travel from place to place to find their daily provisions, and some even had to venture outside into the weather during the process. Whole cities were affected and many built something called Main Street so that the shops could be lined up in a row.

But in those olden days, nobody was more inconvenienced by the absence of malls than the young people, particularly those not yet old enough to drive. There was no designated place for them to meet and play their mating game as they now do in the malls. For practice in the basic human instincts, they had to be creative.

Fortunately, there was something called the box supper. Box suppers were usually once-a-year affairs and did not allow weekly or even daily opportunities as the malls now do. But a box supper was a big enough event that if we handled it properly, we could use up a whole year's worth of mating skills and go through a whole year's supply of emotions in just one short night.

In our small country school, we held the box suppers in the fall, because they were used to raise money to buy Christmas treats for the poor children in the community. But since we were all poor in those days, we all qualified for the free sacks from Santa Claus anyway. The box supper was a community event, and because Friday night television wasn't very good in those days, almost everybody in the community came. The affair always started with a program which allowed the students to demonstrate their various acting and musical talents. As I remember those programs, they were professional revues on par with a good Las Vegas show and just below what you might see on Broadway. I'm sure that as my parents remember them, they were typical children's amateur events with makeshift curtains, forgotten lines, awkward recitals, and more humor growing out of mistakes than intentions. It's funny how age and participation alter our perception of events.

After the program, we held the box auction. All the females in the community, from small girls to grandmothers, had decorated a box. In those days, it was always a shoe box, but since we were in cowboy country, some enterprising ladies used boot boxes. They would wrap the box with crepe paper and bows and ties and other catchy designs. A great deal of creativity and artistic skill went into the decoration of each box, and we were indeed appreciative.

But that decorated box was only the bait, the lure. Those ladies would cook their very finest meal and pack it inside the box. Most of us males learned quite early in life a good lesson of correlation, in that the best-looking box did not always contain the best-tasting food. To this day, I am not all that impressed with packaging, a lesson I learned from going to box suppers.

The ladies carried their boxes in on the sly and stacked them at the front of the schoolhouse. The catch was that nobody knew which lady belonged to which box — or, at least, nobody was supposed to know. Of course, if the couple were going steady, the girl would be sure to point out which box was hers so there would be no mistake for her young man. Also, everybody always knew which box belonged to the teacher. Other than that, it was all so secretive, and during the auction we were to buy a box of supper and, in the process, buy a lady to eat it with us.

The males are not as stupid as the females have been led to believe. We always had our ways of figuring out which box belonged to whom. There were little telltale signs and helpful hints. For one thing, the auctioneer was always a man, and he was on our side. As he held up each box, he would make some smart comment about it, and we would listen for the shriek or watch to see whose cheeks turned red. Then we would know.

Even in those days there were certain mating rituals among the young people, not unlike the mating calls which run through the malls of the land every Friday night nowadays. If some girl had a special interest in you, she would slip up to you during the preliminary program and whisper in your ear which box was hers. This was as close to a Sadie Hawkins proposal as you were ever going to get. It meant that of all the males in the whole universe, this fine lady had chosen you, that you had a special place in her heart, and that she wanted to share her supper and possibly her life with you. Oh, what a thrill it was to get such an offer.

But the intrigue was not finished just because you knew which box to buy. You still had to execute the purchase at public auction. That was the tricky part because of somebody named R.B. Shepherd. R.B. Shepherd was a nice guy and I liked him, except on Box Supper Night. His one major function at the box supper was to run up the bid on boxes that young boys were trying especially hard to buy. He would watch us bid, then laugh and bid even higher. It was a game for him, but for us it was a matter of life or death, or at least life without a mate for supper, which was worse than death. But we boys soon learned tricks of our own. We would bid on boxes which weren't the ones we hoped to buy, just to watch R.B. Shepherd bid. Then, of course, the little girl who had whispered in our ear would turn around and stare at us in that kind of special female stare that I've learned to interpret during thirty-five years of marriage. Then R.B. Shepherd would know he was on a red-herring chase and he would cease bidding until he caught us bidding again. In spite of all that, there was some justice, even in those days. R.B. Shepherd would get caught a few times during the night and would wind up buying four or five boxes. Imagine trying to eat four or five suppers, getting stuffed before you had finished, and trying to decide which lady's dessert you would reject. Let's say that he paid a price for his pranks.

Once you had managed to fool R.B. Shepherd and had bought the box you wanted, you and your lady friend would find a grassy spot out on the playground and sit down to enjoy a picnic under the beautiful starry fall sky. In this romantic environment, the flirting soon began. You would chat and try to be funny, and she would giggle and try to be coy. You would spend much longer eating supper than you ever did before in your life, and when it was all over, you would go home, go to bed, and lie there playing the whole evening over and over in your mind, reading color and tone into every word and motion, and suddenly remembering what you should have said that you didn't say and what you should have done that you didn't do. When the replay was finished, the box supper was then finally over for that year and you waited with anticipation for another year. That was the nature of the mating ritual before there were malls.

But the virtue of that once-a-year event was that the real value and even the real joy was not in the box supper itself, but in the preparation. It took us weeks and months to get ready for the box supper. Of course, we had to prepare our pieces for the program, but that was not the major part. We also had to be schooled in manners and techniques. Our mothers weren't about to let us eat supper with some unknown member of the opposite sex of the community without prior training. This would begin early. At least two months before, mothers across the land would begin to use box supper embarrassment as a motivational tool for etiquette instruction.

"Don't talk with your mouth full. If you talk with your mouth full at the box supper, that girl will think that you're nothing but a country hayseed who just fell off the potato wagon. And eat slowly. Chew each bite forty times. And don't eat mashed potatoes with your fingers. You don't want to make a fool out of yourself."

After Mother got your eating habits corrected, it was then time for the advanced course in how to make small talk with a member of the opposite sex. "Always tell her how nice she looks and how pretty the box is. Remember that she worked hard on that box and she wants to hear that you appreciate it. Notice the little things about it. Don't spend the whole evening talking about yourself. Talk about her and what she's interested in. And if you bog down, you can always say something about the weather and how pretty the sky is. But whatever you do, don't talk about baseball. And don't spend the evening talking to the boy sitting next to you. Give all of your attention to the girl. She worked hard on this supper and she wants this to be a night she can remember."

I always wondered what mothers told their daughters in preparation for the box supper. I suspect it was about the same thing, because it always seemed that we both ate with false manners and engaged in prerehearsed small talk.

Although we had learned our manners and the art of conversation, the major preparation for the box supper was in our own personal anticipation. For weeks, we would lie awake at night and imagine how nice it was going to be and how much fun we were going to have.

How exciting just to plan and to make the mental preparations and to dream dreams! Then the night would come; in a few hours it was over, and we would spend the next few months trying to decide if it was all as much fun as we thought it was going to be.

During the last forty-five years, I've learned that many events in life are like those box suppers of our childhood. There's more fun and excitement and instruction in the preparation than in the event itself. Once I spent some time getting an advanced degree, thinking that it would be fun to have one. But I learned that it was a lot more fun getting the degree than having it. Once I spent some time writing a book, thinking that it would be fun to have written a book. But I learned that it was a lot more fun writing the book than having written it. Once I ran a marathon, thinking it would be fun to run one. But I learned that it was far more fun preparing to run the marathon than running one.

There's a reason for this phenomenon. I call it progress. Life goes forward, and when it quits going forward, life is over. Preparing for a big event is progress, but if the big event is so rewarding and so satisfying and so fulfilling that we spend the rest of our lives basking in the event itself, then life doesn't go anywhere.

I liked box suppers. I got to share the evening with a pretty girl, and that contributed to my education. But the real education was getting ready to do it all over again next year.

I'm glad we didn't have malls.

CHAPTER EIGHT

The Essay Contest

ONE OF THE major challenges of being a parent is to know how to respond to a child's God-given talent. This one factor alone probably accounts for more anxiety and more conflict than any other area of human relationship. As we all know, the biggest sin a parent can commit is to put pressure on a child to meet expectations the child does not have the God-given talent to meet. The second biggest sin a parent can commit is not to put enough pressure on a child and let him waste his God-given gift. Wouldn't parenting be a much simpler enterprise if our children came to us with messages on their foreheads telling us what their gifts were and in what measure they possessed those gifts?

To find that proper balance of pressure and to avoid the risk of being labeled a despot or an uncaring patsy, parents often resort to a variety of methods. Some use what I call the shotgun method, splattering their children's talents all over town in every activity available. They have them in ballet lessons, swimming competition, baton-twirling classes, Little League sports, clubs and orga-

nizations, including the balloon-twisting group, in hopes
that something may have appeal and a rare prodigy will
emerge.

Other parents use a more selective method of the big
whip. They put their children in one activity and threaten
them just to dare not to excel. "This kid's got my genes
in him and he will learn to play baseball if it kills him,"
they report, and they proceed through life with the whip
hanging heavily over the child's head. "What do you
mean stop for ice cream? You just struck out twice in one
game. We'll get ice cream when the batting average goes
up." And the war goes on.

When I was a youth trying desperately to find out if I
had talent in anything, my father used another method. I
call it the car key encouragement method. He used it
only once, but it served its purpose.

My father encouraged me in several activities along the
way. He even encouraged me in some that I wasn't good
at. For example, I was never very athletic; the ugly truth
is that I just wasn't fast. One day I was bemoaning that
fact to my father, and he said, "Well, if you could spend
more time practicing and didn't have to work on this
farm so much, maybe you would be a little better." I
knew that wasn't true and I was rather sure that he knew
it wasn't true either, but I loved him for saying it anyway.
So I worked even harder on the farm.

Once my father went beyond encouragement. He was
a member of an organization called the Farm Bureau,
and although he was not a hard-core member always
attending meetings and pledging his all to it, he still took

some activities rather seriously. One night he came home from a meeting and announced to me that the Farm Bureau was sponsoring an essay contest for high school students. Then he paused, thought for a moment, and in that indirect speech pattern which he used so often, he said, "I'm sure you will want to write an essay for the contest." I knew by that that he wanted me to write the essay. The message was clear. I also knew at that moment that I would write the essay. But I forgot about it and both of us went through life perfectly content with my poor memory—for about two weeks.

That was the night of the big basketball game. A visiting team was coming to town, one of the Harlem Globetrotter clones so popular in those days. They were going to play the best of the local boys, and it would be one exciting evening. All day long every student in school was atingle with the excitement. We couldn't wait for the big night. I hurried home, did my chores as quickly as I could, cleaned up, and went in to ask my father for the car keys so I could go off to see what was probably going to be one of the most significant sporting events of the century. "Sure," he said in a calm, gentle tone, barely looking up from the paper he was reading. "As soon as I see that essay you've written." I was floored, injured, mortally wounded. Despite my protest and my promise of doing better in the future, he never lost his calmness or his focus. "As soon as I see the essay," was all that he would say.

Dejected and embarrassed and even angry, I went back to my room and whipped out that essay—a three-and-one-half page masterpiece about a local farmer who had been killed in a tractor accident because he had been careless just for a moment.

Well, to hasten to the punchline, my essay was judged the champion, and I won five dollars and the honor of reading it to the meeting of the Custer County Farm Bureau. My father came and sat on the front row.

Now, forty years later, I sometimes call myself a professional writer. At least I make a little money at it. When I meet with other professional writers, we often sit around at night and swap stories about how we got started in this madness of self-inflicted pain and agony just to watch words come out of our minds and wind up on paper. Those stories always go back to the first time we ever made any money from the activity, and I tell about the time when my father wouldn't let me have the car keys to go to a basketball game.

My father's method for helping me discover my God-given talent was a little different from those others I mentioned. He didn't make me write that essay because he *hoped* I could if he applied enough threat. He asked me to write the essay because he *knew* I could write it. There was something in his tone which assured me of his confidence. Although I missed the ball game, I still knew that he genuinely believed I could do it and do it well.

Since those days, we have made a science of motivating our children or students or workers. My father didn't know all that much about that science. He just expected us to do it, and we did it. And that's the most powerful motivator of all.

In fact, the scientists themselves have even discovered that factor. A few years ago, researchers divided some students into three random groups. They called in one set of teachers and explained that they were fortunate: that year they were getting the finest students in the school. Another set of teachers were told that they were getting average students. The third set of teachers were told that they would have the worst students. At the end of the year, the students had performed just as the teachers had been told that they would. What the teachers expected to happen did happen.

If we believe in our children, genuinely believe in them so powerfully that they sense our believing, there is a good chance that they are going to do what they can to fulfill our expectations.

As I sit here writing this, it is now late on a Thursday night, but I'm determined to finish before I go to bed. There is an important football game tomorrow night that I would like to see, and the memory of my father looking over my shoulder won't let me stop until I've completed the chapter. Praise God for parents who apply the right kind of pressure.

Chapter Nine

How the Great Glob
Turned to Gold

TIME IS A magnificent healer. Regardless of the ailment, Dr. Time can usually fix it up. Not long ago I had a bout with the flu. When I went to my doctor he said, "If you take a shot and some antibiotics, you can be over this in a week; but if you don't take all that medicine, this stuff is going to last seven whole days." And I knew what he meant. Time heals the flu, broken bones, broken hearts, and bad memories. Praise God for the healing power of time.

Just to show how effectively time heals, I can now eat margarine. In fact, I don't mind margarine. Perhaps my taste buds aren't too sophisticated, but I would just as soon have margarine as real butter. That wasn't always the case.

I first encountered margarine during World War II, and our meeting was not at all pretty. I'm not sure why butter was in short supply, especially out on the farm. I think we must have been sending it overseas for the troops. I do remember that there was a patriotism factor involved. Somehow, if you ate butter, you were an insensitive, disloyal un-American oaf.

So Mom brought this new stuff home from the store. We called it oleo. Since I was the only child around when she returned from her shopping, she asked me to help carry the groceries in and put things away. That's when I met oleo. Completely innocent and unsuspecting, I removed this little package all wrapped up with butcher paper and proceeded to open it for my mom. Suddenly, I came face to face with this ugly glob of horrible-looking, off-white gunk. It just lay there on the table oozing and seeping and looking totally unedible. I remember that it looked like the white hand-cleaner that real mechanics use to get the grease and oil off. To this day, every time I watch a mechanic clean his hands, I have a little trouble ordering a baked potato for supper.

Well, you can gather from all this that oleo was less than an attractive alternative to real butter. Taste buds are funny little fellows that don't work independently of the other senses. If something doesn't *look* edible, it isn't going to *be* edible. So there we were, my mother and I, with this glob of ugly gunk lying there in the middle of the kitchen table. Somehow we had to get it ready for the rest of the family to eat and enjoy. That's when we discovered another little package which had been thrown in — the artificial coloring, a little package of yellow crystals. The transformation would be simple. We would just mix those yellow crystals into that white gunk and presto, we would have a first-class butter substitute. Of course, mixing wasn't all that pleasant either. I had to roll up my sleeves and plunge my hands all the way into that glob, and then I had to knead and push and roll and wrap, but finally, my efforts paid off and the glob took on the appearance of a golden brick. It would have actually been rather pretty, in fact, a thing of beauty, if I hadn't seen it before that artificial junk had been kneaded in.

But the rest of the family didn't know, and they came to the table and ate heartily. Oh, they complained, but I could tell it wasn't all that sincere. "This stuff doesn't taste like real butter," they would say, as they spread great blobs on their bread and scarfed the whole thing down.

As I sat there munching on a dry crust, I watched them merrily eating along, and I resented them. I resented them for what they didn't know and what seemed as if they didn't want to know. So I decided I would tell them all the gory details about how that golden spread was once nothing but an unappealing glob of gunk, and how it got transformed into what they were eating. But then I looked over at my mom, and the expression on her face communicated to me that I really shouldn't tell.

At that moment, even while I was still very young, I learned an important lesson about being a parent. A lot of the success in parenting depends on what secrets you keep. Of course, there are some secrets that you shouldn't keep, but there are some things that your family probably shouldn't know, at least for now.

There was that time when we were one piece of pie short, and Mom said she just wasn't hungry for dessert that night. Then, there was the time when we children won an honor and were going to be decorated in an assembly. Somehow our parents managed to get us new shoes, and we never even knew of the sacrifice they made.

Those are the secrets of successful parenting. Those are the secrets we inherited and pass down to our children, and that they pass on to our grandchildren. Being a parent is one joyous sacrifice, but we keep it to ourselves.

I'm glad for those secrets, because now, all these years later, I can invite my brother and sisters to our house for Christmas dinner and serve them margarine without their once knowing how it got to be such a delicacy. Only my mom and I know, and we still sometimes glance at each other as if we're sharing a secret. But we're not telling.

CHAPTER TEN

Nineteen Hundred Fifty-Seven

NINETEEN HUNDRED FIFTY-SEVEN was a significant year in the history of the United States and the world. That was the year of the major battle of the cold war. The Soviets launched Sputnik.

For me and for most of my generation, the cold war was a scary and a strange war. We didn't fight with planes and guns and bombs. We fought with words and threats and rumors and even jokes. We didn't have television cameras at every corner of the battle site bringing us moment-by-moment reports of the ebb and flow of action, documenting in real pictures the effectiveness of our weaponry and the inefficiency of the enemy. Instead, we made up the pictures in our minds, and deep inside we had no idea whether they were anywhere close to reality. What we didn't know was hurting us.

In this war of words, we made up jokes about the austerity of Soviet life and the failure of the Communist experiment. "Did you hear about the five Russian families who received a picture of Stalin, with instructions to hang it in a prominent place in their home? Four families obeyed, but the fifth did not and was immediately shipped to Siberia. Of course, they couldn't have hung the picture even if they had wanted to, because they lived in the middle of the room."

More from fear than humor, we would laugh heartily and tell ourselves that we had the best life and the best facilities and the best system. Then one day the Soviets launched Sputnik.

Based on our conjectures of what a Russian scientist looked like and what he did in his laboratory, we made up jokes about their silly experiments and their foolish claims that they had invented the wheel and the automobile and anything else that contributed to mankind. Beneath all that laughter, we *knew* that our scientists were better. After all, ours had developed nuclear weapons and knee surgery. There was no way that their scientific achievements and technology were anywhere close to ours. We were far more sophisticated and advanced. Then one day the Soviets launched Sputnik.

As we shopped in our markets stocked with abundance, we made up jokes about the Russians struggling for a loaf of bread and a bowl of borscht. We knew that we had the best life because we had the best system. Logic was on our side. Comfort and the good life were on our side. Economics were on our side. Patriotism and loyalty were on our side. We were the best. There was no doubt about it. Then one day the Soviets launched Sputnik.

To say that this frightened us would be an understatement. Sputnik gripped our nation with a chokehold of fear which almost cut off the blood supply to our brains and rationality. We panicked.

We lost confidence in ourselves and in our system, but we especially lost confidence in our position in the world and in our cold war of words. "Oh, no!" we exclaimed. "What will the neighbors think of us now?"

So we did what Americans always do in the face of crisis. We rolled up our sleeves and went to work. On the possibility that the Soviets had trained better scientists than we had, we reformed the schools. Congress passed the National Defense Education Act, and we spent our money on textbooks instead of tanks. We would catch them in the classroom first; then we would catch them in space. Even our students bought into this. For ten years, every time a student would hold up his hand and ask that ageless and ever-present student question, "Why are we doing this, anyway?" the teacher would answer tersely and emphatically, with strains of "The Star-Spangled Banner" floating through his mind, "Because we are catching up with the Russians. That's why."

The student would say, "Oh," and would get back to his work of factoring and figuring square root as his patriotic duty.

With motivation accounted for, we broke into new math and linguistics and lab sciences and homework. We had to catch up. After overhauling the schools, we went to work preparing our communities. We dug holes in the ground and stuck in metal tanks and called them bomb shelters. We filled our bomb shelters and basements with canned food and bottled water; then we posted a sign somewhere announcing how many people could live on those supplies in the event of an attack.

Whole communities got into the act by having community-wide emergency practice days. We took a day off from all other activities—school, work, and shopping—and we all practiced our roles of what we would do if there were a major emergency. We drove ambulances and carried the fake injured to high school gyms where we treated their wounds and put them to bed on cots. We posted guards on the outskirts of town, and we memorized a map of where all the shelters were. In retrospect, I remember the exercise as fun, but we went about it all rather somberly. In this war of words and fears where neither side knew how the other was armed, we didn't take anything for granted. We never knew when the big battle might take place. We just knew we had to be prepared.

To make matters even worse, the leader from the other side visited our country a few years later. With his well-nourished physique, and his hearty enthusiasm for the Soviet way, he came to the United Nations where he proceeded to take off his shoe and beat his message out on the table before him. "We will bury you," Mr. Krushchev told us, and frankly, he sounded rather persuasive. The problem was that we didn't know whether or not they could do it, so we worked on the theory that they could. But could this be possible? Could this nation of bad guys who didn't believe in God actually bury us, the good guys? "Naw," we said to ourselves. "It could never happen." In response to that, we created a new fear—the fear that our system would crumble from within. And we began to look for Communist conspirators in every nook and cranny. One of my favorite television programs in those days, full of intrigue, suspense, and fear, was about an FBI undercover agent who infiltrated Communist cell groups and broke up their subterfuge. It was good drama each week; but more than that, it was a reminder to us all to be vigilant.

So what is the summary of all this some thirty years later? Well, the ideology that sent a shoe-banging Communist to the U.N. with the threat to bury us crumbled from within. Our system of shopping malls and daily newspapers and forty television channels and superhighways and a motto of "In God We Trust" is still going strong.

Don't spend too long searching for a profound point in my reporting of this. I'm not sure I have one, unless it would be surprise. In 1991 Mary and I went off to live for a year in the empire that once wrought so much fear in our hearts, and we were treated with abundant kindness and graciousness. Our children, who are young adults now, could never quite comprehend our fascination by it all, but we have to keep in mind that our children have never been in a bomb shelter, have never practiced community emergency procedures, have never seen an episode of "I Was a Communist for the F.B.I.," and didn't feel the effects of Sputnik.

I once heard a story which, if it isn't true, should be. Legend tells us that when Benjamin Franklin finally emerged from that lengthy committee meeting where our forefathers had hammered out the Constitution, someone stopped him and asked, "What have you given us?"

According to the story, Franklin said, "We have given you a republic. Now the challenge is to see if you can keep it." I wonder if Franklin knew the wisdom of his words. The most obvious point is that keeping the republic is a continuous battle. Every generation must win whatever battle comes to it, but every generation must win some battle. In our generation, we won the cold war. It seems to me that we need to be rather diligent in telling our children about that.

In this country we sometimes bask in our weaknesses, and even exaggerate to make the most of them. Maybe it's time that we bask in some of our strengths. I have heard a lot of guesses about why the Soviet Union crumbled—American military buildup, careless accidents such as Chernobyl, or corruption in the party. Maybe all of these are true, and maybe none of them. Maybe the reason for all this change is the simple matter that despite all its flaws and problems, our system works and theirs didn't. Maybe that's the real lesson of the cold war.

But the year of 1957 carried another message to Americans, one that's too important to ignore. During that year some more news came to us from closer to home. The military regime down in the little island of Cuba had apparently been taking advantage of the people, abusing human rights, and the people needed a change—liberation from tyranny and persecution. In short, they needed a revolution.

The revolution came—in the person of a dynamic young leader named Fidel Castro. He was a dashing figure, almost a character out of a romantic novel; and he captured the imagination and support of many Americans. Hiding out in the wilderness and striking at appropriate times, he led the people through a successful revolt and brought many cheers from this country. The television crews hurried to Havana for interviews and scoops; and soon Castro's face, with the cigar hanging out of one corner of his mouth, was almost as familiar to us as George Washington's.

Since this is not a history book, I won't document the steps Castro took in moving from America's ideal of the romantic hero to public enemy number one, but it is now obvious that he took those steps. The point is not that we were all fooled by Castro. Instead, the point is that we need to understand the character of revolution itself.

Lesser revolutions take place every day in some form or another, but too often we don't understand them, and that misunderstanding leads to chaos and heartbreak. Revolutions are always two-directional. We revolt against something, and, at the same time, revolt toward something. We can never allow ourselves to get so caught up in the first direction that we lose sight of the second.

Just consider the revolutions throughout history. The Russians turned away from the czars and got the Bolsheviks. That's no bargain. The French turned away from the Louis and got Napoleon. That's no bargain. Cuba turned away from Batista and got Castro. That's no bargain.

Somehow we have to account for both directions.

We see this played out in some form almost every day. The church decides that it must get rid of the present pastor. There is a real problem, for which the pastor is deemed responsible, and they must move away from this pastor as quickly as they can. So they send the first person packing, and then spend three years searching for a replacement. In the meantime, about fifty percent of the people wander off to other churches, the offering drops to a paltry sum, and the parking lot crumbles. What a sorry sight, this aftermath of one-directional revolution!

I know men who one day woke up and decided that they needed to get rid of their present wife. Whatever the problem, it was insurmountable and unsolvable, and the only choice was to follow through the revolution of getting rid of the tyranny that plagued them. So they dumped the first wife and woke up the next day realizing that they couldn't live without a wife. They hurried into a search, found a poor substitute for the first wife, and lived the rest of their lives wondering what they did to deserve such misery.

That's the lesson we learned from Cuba in 1957. Don't throw away what you've got, until you know that what you're going to get in its place is going to be better.

CHAPTER ELEVEN

Backyard Baseball

"YOU'RE ONLY AS old as you feel," the adage tells us. I'm not really sure I know what that means, but as I get older, I have come to realize that age is relative. To tell someone that you're sixty years old doesn't communicate as much about you as to tell someone that you're sixteen.

One of the methods I use to ascertain the relative age of a person is the word-association technique. The image that immediately comes to your mind at the mention of certain words definitely dates you. A great example of that is the term Youth Baseball. If that phrase makes you think of a whole group of children playing on a lighted, manicured field while wearing expensive uniforms complete with fielding gloves, batting gloves, and fancy helmets, and being coached by experienced adults who take their responsibility very seriously while being cheered on by stands full of screaming, irrational parents, then you're a youngster.

If Youth Baseball reminds you of a few kids out in the backyard swinging a bat with "Mickey Mantle" written on it, sharing gloves between innings because there were only half enough to go around, and throwing a Christmas-present baseball which was new and nice until the night you left it out in the rain and it shriveled and turned brown, then you are middle-aged.

On the other hand, if Youth Baseball drives you to a memory of a small group of boys swinging a bat made from a tree limb and hitting a ball made out of a marble wrapped in twine with a denim cover sewed on, then you're so old that you really shouldn't put all your candles on your birthday cake, because that would create a fire hazard.

Although I played some of the latter kind of youth baseball, most of my career was spent in the game of the middle-aged. In those days, baseball was always played with two shortages—a shortage of people and a shortage of space.

There weren't eighteen people in our whole community who had time to stop and play baseball all afternoon, so we always played with less than full teams. That provoked us to creativity, and we invented rules to accommodate the number of players we had.

One of our created games was a sport we called Crossover. Because we didn't have enough people to man the bases, we could get runners out by throwing the ball in front of them as they ran from base to base; thus, the name Crossover. Crossover games were fun except for the ending, since they always ended in a crying match. Sometime during the waning moments, particularly if the score was a little lopsided, some base runner would get hit with the ball during a Crossover maneuver. That brought accusations and tears.

"You did that on purpose, boo hoo."

"Did not."

"Did too. I'm telling Momma."

"It was your fault anyway. You were running too fast. Real players don't run that fast."

The war of words mingled with tears would go on, signifying that the game was finished. The one thing I did notice was that the person who got hit was always on the team that was winning.

The other sport we invented for a limited number of players was Indian Ball. I have no idea why we gave it that name. In Indian Ball, we designated a small space for the playing field, and we had to hit the ball to specified spots for point value. That taught us concentration and batting skills.

The shortage of space also caused us to be creative. There was never enough room in the backyard for us to have a full field, so we worked long and hard to engineer an effective stadium with what was available.

By putting things on an angle, we could usually get first base a good distance from home plate. Often first base was almost regulation distance. And first base itself was something permanent like a hubcap or a flat rock. Second base was a shorter distance and it was temporary—such as a piece of cardboard. Third base was about three steps from first base and was as temporary as a tuft of grass.

Backyard baseball necessitated very involved field rules

which were carved in stone and never varied throughout the years. If you hit the ball into the rosebushes, you had an automatic double, and had to wait at second base for a long time, because extricating a baseball from a rosebush is not a task to be performed in haste.

If you hit the ball anywhere toward the McElmurrys' yard, you were automatically out. Mr. McElmurry was the superintendent of schools, and we didn't want to have to go over to his yard and try to persuade him to give our ball back.

Even the shape and size of the field took on a certain sacredness through the years. When we had worn the grass away and had caused ruts for base paths, our parents came out and suggested that we change the field and wear the grass away somewhere else. We tried that; we really did. But the national pastime just wasn't the same on that newly designed field which demanded new ground rules and new running directions. So we quickly scrapped that plan and went back to the old proven field with ruts for base paths.

In baseball, you just don't mess with tradition.

Despite the glitz, glamor, and professionalism of the modern Youth Baseball, the older edition had some definite advantages. For one thing, in the backyard, you got to use your imagination. In your imagination, you could make the stadiums bigger and filled with fans. You could have more striking uniforms, and you could make the catcher gear any color you wanted it to be.

And you could be somebody famous. We never played under our own names. In fact, you might remember me from my playing days. My name was Alvin Dark. I stood like Alvin Dark. I swung like Alvin Dark, and when I hit the ball, I took that big turn around first base like Alvin Dark. I not only had his moves, at times I almost thought I was Alvin Dark. And I played with people named Mantle and Maris and Mayes, so I really didn't stand out from the amateurs. If we had enough people to have a catcher, which wasn't all that often, he was always Campy. Every catcher who ever played on our field was Campy.

How can kids in the real uniforms, playing in front of stands full of parents, with coaches supervising every move, imagine that they are actually smaller versions of their favorite diamond stars? The game isn't the same.

The other advantage to the backyard sport was that we never kept score. At least, we never published it in the paper, and we had forgotten who won by what margin when it was time to play the next day. We say that the children of today "play" baseball, but can it really be "play" if they put the score in the paper for everyone to see and pick a champion when the summer is over? That all sounds rather serious to me.

A couple of summers ago I was driving through Suburbia, U.S.A. on a hot, lazy July afternoon, when I turned a corner and came on the most remarkable sight I've seen in years—a relic from the past. A true museum piece. Five boys and a girl were running around in the middle of a vacant lot, hitting balls into rosebushes and running bases in ruts a foot deep.

As best as I could judge, it looked as if they were having fun.

CHAPTER TWELVE

The Plow

I WAS FOUR years old when the Japanese bombed Pearl Harbor, so I don't remember all that much about World War II. In my imagination, some German soldiers camped out down behind the boulders along our creek. I shot at them once in a while with my finger gun; and I sent some real live ammo their way the time my older brother let me play with his rubber rifle, but they were too cowardly to show themselves, so I didn't help the Allied effort all that much.

I did help plant the victory gardens at school, and I collected tin cans. The only time I remember going to a movie, I stood and sang as much of "The Star-Spangled Banner" as I knew by heart.

Other than that, my real memory of the war centered on the nice lady who lived down the road from us. Because she didn't live too far away and because the road didn't have cars on it, her house was within the range of my designated traveling area, and I would go to see her on a regular basis. I went because I liked her, but I also went because of the popcorn. She made the best popcorn. She would go into her pantry and get these ears of corn out of a gunnysack. Then she would sit and shell the corn into a bowl that she held in her lap. After she had shelled the corn, she needed my help. She would hold the corn up high and let it trickle through her hands back into the bowl. While it was trickling down, I had to blow on it to send the chaff away. Mine was an important role in the whole process. I have no idea how that lady made popcorn when I wasn't there to blow on it for her.

After I had blown all the chaff away, she would pop that corn in an old black skillet, and just the memory of the aroma in the house is enough to make me drool, even to this day.

On her front door, the nice lady had a big chart that was all decorated in patriotic colors, and it had three big stars all around it. At the time I didn't know what all that meant, although I knew it had something to do with the war. Since it didn't affect the taste of the popcorn, I wasn't eager to find out.

One day as I was making my rounds, I dropped by her house, and that display board with the patriotic colors and the three stars was covered by a big black wreath. I knew that had something to do with the war too, but I didn't really understand it all. When I knocked, the nice lady came out, and I could see that she had been crying. She hugged me and told me that she didn't feel like making popcorn; so I went away sad, not because of the popcorn as much as because she was sad.

A few days later, our plow wore out. It didn't really

break—it just wore out. Sometimes things wear out, even when it's inconvenient for them to do so, as in the middle of a war when everything is in scarce supply anyway. But our plow wore out, and we had to have a new one. There was no choice.

I went with my dad to the plow shop. A chubby, grinning man came out to greet us. He was dressed in smart-looking khakis, and he had on a leather bow tie which must have been too small, because his face was all red like he was short on air.

The grinning man showed us the plows, and he had exactly what we needed. But when he told us the price, my dad just shook his head, stared at the ground, and said, "That's three times more than it's worth."

The man never lost his grin. He nodded agreement and said, "I know it, but there's a war on. You have to have a plow. I'm the only man in town who has one. If you want the plow, you'll pay my price."

Then I realized something. That man with the tie that didn't fit didn't care about that nice lady who was too sad to make popcorn. She was someone else's problem. In fact, he was happy the war was going on, and he wasn't all that eager to see it end.

I am sorry that this lesson is true. I'm sorry I had to learn it in such a way. But I'm glad I know it.

CHAPTER THIRTEEN

Parenting and Indirect Speech

IN 1991, MARY and I went to the Ukraine for the purpose of teaching Ukrainian English teachers how to speak English properly. Anyone who has ever heard me speak immediately knows the irony in this. Suffice it to say that I lived in Oklahoma far too long to have a standard American-English approach to oral communication. If you ever go to the Ukraine and hear people saying, "Y'all," "Down yonder," and "Far station," you will know where they learned their English.

During our year of teaching in the Ukraine, one of the significant lessons dealt with indirect speech. Frankly, many Americans haven't thought that much about indirect speech. It is such a natural course of communication for us that we never stop to think about what we are doing when we say to our dinner guests, "Would you like to wash your hands before we eat?"

But for a person who has learned English out of a textbook instead of through the bars of a crib, indirect speech is a major, sophisticated, and difficult component of learning to speak the language like a native.

In all humility, I must admit that I was a rather good teacher for this lesson. I've had a lot of experience with indirect speech. My dad was a master at it. As I think back, it seems to me that many parents in those days had some expertise in the art form and were not afraid to use it. Perhaps they knew more about child psychology back then than we do now.

For one thing, indirect speech is the language of persuasion, far more effective than direct orders barked out at high volume. On Saturdays as we were drawing to the end of breakfast, my dad would lean back in his chair and say, "Well, if you really felt like it, you could spend the day plowing the forty acres." Amazingly enough, I always felt like it. In fact, plowing that forty acres was the very thing I had wanted to do that day. That's what I had been planning to do all week. Never once did I find out what form of address my father would have used if I hadn't felt like plowing that day.

But his ploy of giving assignments with a qualifier was only the beginning of his deployment of sophisticated motivational psychology. One day he came into the house where I was resting a bit from the hot sun, and said, "If you were a little older, a little bigger, and a little stronger, I would ask you to go out and unload that load of hay." Immediately I grew in stature and attitude, and I literally ran out of that house to demonstrate to him once and for all that I was indeed bigger and stronger than he thought I was. Maybe the reason our parents used more indirect speech than we do is that kids were more stupid and easier to fool back in the good old days.

But my dad used that "If you were bigger and stronger" bit on me all the time, and I was twenty-one years old before I realized that I was being tricked.

Indirect speech is not only a tool of motivation; it has correctional value as well. Once when I was still rather small, I brought home a report card which was a little worse than I had been accustomed to. Although our parents never said much to us about our grades, I was still dreading the ordeal of acquiring the required parent signature. I was hoping to find my mother in a good mood and get the whole mess taken care of quickly, but she was busy baking bread, and the one thing we never interrupted was Mom baking bread. She was an artist at it, and artists need the space to produce the kind of art that will melt in your mouth, especially when it is doctored up with a ton of fresh butter and homemade grape jam.

So Dad casually fell into the task of signing our report cards that evening. When he came to mine, he studied it a bit, never changed expression, and commented, "Well, at least you're not cheating." That was enough. My goofing off in class and my doing homework without giving it proper attention had just ended. Nothing he could have said would have been more effective than that one simple statement, spoken almost without emotion. I had been corrected and I knew it.

Breaking curfew was another event which brought the most berating outburst of indirect speech any person could ever endure. I would come home later than I had promised to. My dad would be sitting in the living room reading the book I had checked out of the library to read myself if I ever got around to it, and he, without even looking up, as if he were riveted on a really interesting passage, would say, "Did your watch stop?" This was the most exquisite kind of cruel and unusual punishment, because inside that little question is the implication that my dad believed in me so much that I would never disappoint him intentionally. The only possible reason for my being late would surely have to be some circumstance beyond my control. I had been corrected and I knew it.

Finally, one evening, in his typical indirect fashion, he went straight for the jugular of my moral integrity, and I was never late again. When I came home tardy, he never looked up from his book, but said, "I'm not going to ask you where you've been, because then you would have to lie to me and I'm too proud a man to be the father of a lying son." That was it. No more tardies for me. I just couldn't stand the intensity of the punishment.

As a tool of correction, indirect speech has an added dimension of a haunting nature. Those little indirect statements which border on wit get lodged somewhere in your memory and keep bursting back in full and vivid recall at the most inappropriate times in the future. I borrowed the car to drive into town, telling my dad that I had to go to a party at church. He agreed, particularly when I made him think that I had a noble purpose. But in those days, going to town required several trips up and down Main Street and other alternate journeys which made my driving around entirely necessary.

The next morning, Dad got into the car, took a glance at the odometer, and said, "Well, I see that they moved the town farther away since the last time I was there." I knew then that I had not only been corrected for my past deeds, but I had been corrected from any future abuse of my driving privileges. Every time a kid at church would ask me to take him somewhere several miles out of my way, I would think of that one little statement about the moving of the town, and I would politely decline.

Indirect speech can also be employed to help parents make that most very difficult statement of parenthood — the one where you are disappointed in what your child has done, but your child is also disappointed in himself, maybe even more than you are. You need to express your disappointment, but you need to do it in such a way that you don't do damage to a person who is already vulnerable from wrestling with a load of guilt. Let me tell you how my dad handled that with me.

One evening while I was out on a date and being silly, I ran into a mailbox. Although this was not a serious demolition accident, it did cause some ugly bumps and wrinkles in the family car. I was scared, to say the least. No sixteen-year-old looks forward to going home and telling his parents that he has turned their beautiful machine into a pile of ugly metal. But more than being scared, I was sad. I had done something wrong, and I had absolutely no excuse. Oh, how I played the accident over and over in my mind, wishing in every way that I hadn't done it. But it was reality. The bumps and wrinkles were there, and I had to face it. I found my father sitting in the living room reading a book as usual. I explained to him what had happened, not really wanting him to hit me and slap me, but somehow hoping that he would, just so I could get out from under that pile of guilt I was carrying around.

Again he never looked up so that I might read the disappointment in his face. He only said, "I think that they should pass a law against these moving mailboxes. They are so hard to miss when you're out driving, particularly when you've got your arm around some girl."

Notice that it isn't always the quantity of words that communicates. It's the quality too. Jesus knew this. One day He said to His disciples, "Whom do people say that I am?" That was an innocent little question and the disciples really got into it. They gave a rather thorough report, each speaking his mind openly and completely. And when they had finished blurting out their answers, Jesus said, "Whom do you say that I am?" Fourteen words. That's all you need. Just fourteen words to make your message coherent, comprehensive, and unforgettable.

I've even been doing some research on my own. Several years ago, we had a serious snowstorm. The next morning I woke my preadolescent son and said, "Now don't try to shovel this. You're too young to shovel all this snow by yourself." When I came home that night, the drive and sidewalks were beautifully clear. Last spring we had a major blizzard. I went in and said to Mary, "You're too pretty and too refined to shovel snow." And with that she said, "Bet your life on it, Buster, and if you think that cheap trick of indirect speech is going to work on me, you're dumber than I thought you were."

Maybe it's in the tone we use.

CHAPTER FOURTEEN

Dr. Mom

BACK IN THE good old days, one of the prerequisites for motherhood was to be board-certified in family medical practice and to have credentials in veterinary medicine as well, if the family had pets. Although Mom's clinic and apothecary were not as well stocked and didn't smell the same as the official ones, we nevertheless recovered from most of our maladies with only minor lasting effects.

To achieve family health, Mom used three kinds of treatment: packs, potions, and soaks. Sometimes she would prescribe a single dosage, but most of the time she used all three together.

Although my mom was not as specialized in packs as some other moms, she still understood the basic concept and employed it often. Packs could be concocted from about anything, as long as they met the one criterion of smelling bad. Of course, that was Mom's way of heading off epidemics of contagious diseases. When she got that pack on you, it didn't matter whether you went out in public. As bad as you smelled, no one was coming close enough to catch anything anyway.

The most famous packs were poultices used to draw out of you what shouldn't have been in you. In the southwest, we spoke that word with a lazy "t" and called them polluses. Poultices were used to doctor about anything from snakebites to boils to stickers to staph infections. They were made from a variety of materials collected from past research and Mom's imagination. Some people used raw bacon as an effective pack. My mom used bread and milk with sugar in it.

For some poultices, such as those for bee stings, Mom used mud packs. In our day, mud packs were made from dirt and water.

The most powerful packs were those that were supposed to heal by penetrating through your skin and into the ailing part of your body. As I said before, what penetrated was a foul odor. We used Ben Gay, Vicks, hog fat, mustard plaster, onion plaster, and some other stuff I never learned to spell.

Potions were not my mom's area of specialty either, but she could manage. Just as packs had to smell bad, potions had to taste bad. The more horrible the taste, the more hurried the healing. The most obvious and least creative example was castor oil. Whatever happened to castor oil, anyway? I haven't heard of the stuff in years. Readers who watched "Thirtysomething" on TV are saying, "What's castor oil?" Let me answer that question as all the older readers shout, "Amen." It is a magic potion that contains miraculous healing powers from its ability to make you gag when you swallow it. Castor oil was an effective medicine because if you didn't get to feeling better immediately, you lied about it. How many days I woke up in a difficult dilemma: I really didn't feel well enough to go to school, but I was definitely too sick to stay home and take castor oil. Experts who study school attendance patterns should examine the relationship between their figures and the decline of castor oil sales. Frequently, I hear some famous person telling us that the children of today need more heroes, more discipline, more exercise, more snow. Well, I think they need more castor oil. There is no stronger motivation to good health and good morals than a mom with a teaspoon in one hand and a bottle of castor oil in the other.

But castor oil was just a beginning. Those homemade potions didn't come formed into the shape of cartoon characters and doctored with cherry flavoring either. Those with lemon in them were merely foul. Others were hideous, and some, such as kerosene and sugar mixed together for a wonderful nightcap, were downright contemptible. Germs literally ran from your body, just to escape that stuff squishing through your system.

But of all of the therapies available, my mom's specialty area was soaks. She could soak any part of your anatomy in about any solution and make it well. Salts, water, hot milk, and vinegar were always good, but the old standby, the elixir of the cure-alls was a good soak in kerosene. Any open sores or puncture wounds, such as those made by stepping on rusty nails, required an immediate and lengthy kerosene soak. This was both healing medicine and preventive medicine. You had to soak in kerosene to keep from getting lockjaw.

Now there's a disease for you—lockjaw. That sounds like a disease. In the good old days, diseases sounded like diseases. Just the name was enough to stimulate dread and pain. We had lockjaw, croup, sleeping sickness, and hoof-and-mouth disease.

Not long ago I went to see a doctor, and he diagnosed my ailment as extended ligament syndrome. Now what kind of disease is that? There is no way that *syndrome* comes anywhere close to describing the pain in my knee.

In doctoring human ailments, Mom's practice had certain limitations. As far as I know, she never attempted major surgery. But her animal practice was much more daring. One time we had a dog who chased cars. That was not unusual—almost everybody had a dog who chased cars. But most of them did it for sport. Our dog seemed to chase cars with a sense of mission. He chased them as if he had a plan for what to do with the machine, should he ever catch it. Well, one day while chasing a small Jewel Tea truck, he went too far, fell under a wheel, and came out with a broken hind leg. Mom never even asked for the rubber gloves. She went right to work, made a splint out of old roof shingles, bound it together by ripping up my last year's underwear and had that dog chasing cars again the next day. I must admit that it did amuse some of our visitors to be chased by a three-legged dog. Once the colt got caught in the fence and tore a huge hole in his leg. Mom took out her sewing needle and some thread and had him put back together so fine that it didn't even leave a scar.

The thing that I found amazing about Mom's medical

practice is how professionally she went about it. When we would get an injury or an illness, Mom went to work calmly, coolly, and immediately, as if she had doctored at least a thousand such cases. She went about her work with so much poise that we couldn't help but have full confidence in her knowledge and ability, and we probably got well largely because we believed in our doctor.

Only later, when we had time to think about it, would we realize that we were the only children she had ever had. She was making it all up as she went, and that's the secret to successful doctoring and mothering. Make them think you know what you're doing.

I have never seen a wedding where the parents sat around and said, "Well, these two certainly know what they're doing." Isn't it funny how we doubt that the next generation will be creative enough or bold enough to cope, when they take over the world and have to solve crises?

I wonder what my mom's parents and older siblings thought when they heard that she was going to have her first child. I wonder if they said, "Oh, no, what does she know about doctoring a sick child?"

But any of us who ever wore a garlic patch or drank kerosene and sugar or escaped the dreaded lockjaw will tell you that moms are pretty crafty people when they have to be.

Chapter Fifteen

The Telephone

MY MOM TELLS a fascinating story about her father who moved his young family from Kansas to homestead in the Oklahoma Territory. About a year or so later, he sent my grandmother and their young children back to Kansas for a visit with the relatives. Another homesteading family was making the trip, and they had room for my grandmother in their wagon.

It was in the spring, and when they came to the Cimarron River about one hundred miles from home, they found the river too high to cross in the wagon. For two weeks my grandmother and her babies, along with the other family, camped by the side of the river, waiting for the waters to subside. After that they went on to Kansas for their month-long visit.

All this time, my grandfather was back down on the farm in Oklahoma without any word, or any way to even begin to communicate with his family, should there be an emergency. I'm not talking about ancient times when Marco Polo traveled to Mongolia and discovered silk and rice. This is my mother's story. This is less than one lifetime ago. Whenever I think of the telephone and the changes in communication, I can only be amazed.

The first telephone I remember was the Hello, Central variety. We were on a party line with seven other families. This made for interesting rules in telephone etiquette. The telephone apparatus itself, a big wooden box attached to the wall, was always placed in the most conspicuous spot in the house. I always thought that was because it would be more convenient, but I have also come to realize that the location cut down considerably on eavesdropping on the other parties. It was rather difficult to secretively hold a receiver to your ear in the middle of the kitchen while your mom was cooking supper.

If we wanted to talk to somebody, we put the receiver to our ear and listened to see if the line was clear. If we heard people talking, we merely hung up the receiver and waited for a few minutes to try again. How long it took us to listen to see if someone else was on the line depended on several factors. First, it depended on who was talking and the nature of the conversation. If it sounded like something we should know about, we usually held the receiver to our ear a bit longer before we could convince our hand to move it back to the cradle.

The other factor that figured in the length of our listening was how long those two people had been talking. The first time we picked up the receiver and found that the line was not clear, we were the model of courtesy and good manners. We hung up immediately. But if those two were still on the line ten minutes later, we just decided that those brazen busybodies had no right to private business, and we just listened until they were finished, not even caring if they should discover that they had an eavesdropper.

Our telephone service back then was rather sophisticated for the times. We could dial direct to the other seven families on our line. We dialed with a crank which we turned vigorously. We had a code system which usually consisted of some combination of three rings, and we all knew which call was ours by the code. For example, our ring was two shorts and a long. Another family would have two longs and a short.

If we wanted to call anybody other than those people on our line, we had to call Central. Central was always one long ring. When somebody would answer, we would say, "Hello, Central," and then we would tell the operator whom we wished to speak to. In those days, we didn't have numbers. We made telephone calls with names. Telephone numbers themselves are rather amazing little hints of modernity.

Telephone operators were always women, frequently young girls entering the work force in their first jobs. I remember one day in the mid 1970s when I needed assistance and got a male operator for the first time. Despite his kindness and efficiency, my first impulse was still to ask for a real operator. I feel that one of the major achievements in my life is that I have grown to the point that I can do business with a male operator with total trust and confidence.

In smaller communities, Central was more than a telephone exchange. It was also an information emporium. You could call Central and get the time or the date or the hospital admission list or several other little tidbits of current news.

That was the nature of our telephone service. We thought it was probably as fine as it was ever going to get. After all, there had to be some inherent limit to technological progress. Just to have Central was way beyond what my grandfather could have even imagined, when his family was camped at the Cimarron River.

Great changes came to our lives through that magic box hanging in the kitchen. Telephone service was indeed service, and it changed our lives dramatically. The telephone even crept into our worship experience. In those days, one of our gospel songs was a familiar favorite filled with theology and reverence and called "The Royal Telephone." Surely you haven't forgotten this fine song. If it is not a regular feature in your church, perhaps you could tell the minister of music about it and he could correct the oversight. Just consider the sheer beauty and inspiration of the first stanza.

Central's never busy, always on the line.

You can get through to Heaven, almost anytime.

That was the way it was during our youth and we thought forever. But one day something strange happened. Our telephones changed. They told us it was progress, and we accepted it. Instead of boxes on the wall, we had black rotary machines which were pretty enough to be put into the living room as a decorator piece. Incidentally, they also contributed to lengthening our conversations. We could now sit in the comfort of a favorite chair instead of standing on one leg in the middle of the kitchen. We replaced Hello, Central with seven-digit numbers, and we could call all over the community without any assistance. Oh, what a sense of freedom we had! We reduced the number of families on a line from eight to four, and those families who lived in the progressive, uppity sections of town had their very own private lines. Surely, now we had arrived at the ultimate of telephone service. There was no way that technology would ever get any better than this.

A few years later, we added three more numbers, the area code, to our already numbered identity, allowing us to dial direct anywhere in the whole country. Think about that. You could just pick up your phone, ring ten numbers, and talk to Aunt Mabel way out in California as clear as if she were in the next room. It was truly amazing.

A short time later came the push button phones which played little tunes to us as we dialed, and before we could figure out how any of it worked, we had answering machines, portable phones that traveled with us anywhere, and fax machines. Now we have progressed to the point that complete government offices are staffed only by telephones, and where no real person has been employed for years.

The telephone people tell me that very soon I will have a little talking television set so that I can actually see the person with whom I'm speaking. Once in my life I would have doubted that, but not anymore. If they say they can make such a gadget and put it into our homes and hands, I'm sure they can. I'm a true believer.

But I still have one nagging question. Now that I can pick up a phone and dial anybody I want to anywhere in the whole world, and immediately have a meaningful conversation with that person, do I love my family any more than my grandfather loved his, when they were camped up on the Cimarron without any method of contact?

Praise God for the technology which enables us to reach our loved ones and express that love in a moment's notice. But technology is not communication. It is only the tool of communication. If I have no love to give to my wife, there is really no need to call her on the phone, even if it is convenient.

I spend some of my mental energy thinking about a certain television star. For years, he nightly communicated with twenty million people. He was so warm and so genuine and so real that we all thought we knew him personally, and we loved him. Yet, during all this time, he had four wives. Apparently, he was more effective at communicating with twenty million people than he was in talking with his wives.

Interestingly enough, we can go to a class and learn how to communicate with twenty million people. There are rules for that kind of thing. But where are the rules that tell us how to have an honest, mutually communicative conversation with a thirteen-year-old daughter?

Every time the telephone rings and jars me from a deep conversation with a friend or draws me away from

the pages of an Edgar Lee Masters poetry book or inter-
rupts a tender moment with Mary, I pause to wonder if
we really are in charge of our tools or are their victims.

I am reminded of a story once told about the bachelor
farmer who lived by himself a few miles from us. One
night he had visitors and the phone began to ring. When
one of the guests asked in that tone of voice that is more
a command than a question, "Aren't you going to answer
that?" the farmer replied, "I got that contraption for *my*
convenience. Not theirs."

CHAPTER SIXTEEN

The Switching

WHEN I WAS four years old, my brother and I were out playing on the back porch. I had a hammer in my hand, and somehow that hammer managed to find a landing place on my brother's head. My memory is a bit fuzzy here. I'm not sure I know how that happened, but I do remember that my brother was not at all amused. My mother hurried out and immediately flew into her doctor role, applying the packs and potions, but she didn't punish me. She might have screamed, but she didn't punish. There is a difference between being screamed at and being really punished.

But then Daddy came home. That is the inevitable story of my life. Daddy came home. He inspected the injury to my brother's head, ascertained no permanent damage, and then came to me to administer the proper punishment.

He explained very clearly that my action merited a switching. Since he was not into model railroads, I soon deduced what he had in mind. The two of us walked hand in hand out to the backyard in pursuit of the perfect switch. At this point, my dad involved me in the hunt, and soon I was engrossed in this business of finding the proper instrument for my beating. In fact, I became so involved in the search that my father went over and sat in the old tire which served as our swing.

I would bring various candidates for his inspection and each time would get a better definition of specifications. One stick had a knot on it and that would hurt me. One had a thorn on it and that would hurt him. Another was too brittle and would break. Another was too limber and wouldn't sting enough. With his direction and my enthusiasm, I finally located the ultimate tool with which to inflict bodily pain upon a four-year-old boy.

And when I found it after all my effort, my dad rewarded me by giving me the worst switching I have ever had in my life — and the last. He never spanked me again.

I don't know where my dad learned this technique. I don't know whether he was an astute enough child psychologist that he invented it on his own, or if someone had told him about it, but I remember it as an effective measure.

I am sometimes amused at some of the clichés we parents use on our children. "This is going to hurt me worse than it's going to hurt you," we tell them, just as we are gritting our teeth and attempting to inflict as much bodily harm as we can.

But that day there was something in my dad's demeanor that suggested that maybe it did hurt him as much as it did me. One thing I know was that I was not being switched out of some violent response. The whole thing was studied, deliberate, and planned right to perfection.

We parents tell our children, "I am going to punish the deed but not the person," and our children wonder why they hurt so much when it's all over. That day my dad made me feel like an important person, mature enough to assist in a strategic mission; yet, all the while, the mission was punishing me for acting in a childish and irresponsible manner.

At times I allow myself to be put into situations where someone mistakenly assumes that I know something about the awesome and mysterious task of rearing children. Invariably, in the course of the conversation, the person will ask, "Do you think a parent should ever spank a child?"

That's not a simple question to be settled with a yes or no answer. But I enjoy it anyway because while I'm formulating a complex answer, ambiguous enough to leave them wondering what I'm saying, I run through my mind the pleasant memories of that warm spring evening years ago, when my dad and I found the perfect switch needed to remind me that I shouldn't hit people on the head with hammers.

CHAPTER SEVENTEEN

When Company Came

"TRAVEL BROADENS YOU," our teachers told us, but what they didn't tell us is that there are two ways to further our education through travel. We can pack up, leave our homes, and venture forth on our own. Or we can stay in the security and comfort of our own homes, and play hosts to the company who comes from far-off and exotic lands.

We were native Oklahomans, and the company that came to our house were the cousins from California. Just their coming and telling us of life there was about as exotic and alien as we could stand. I'm not sure we would have actually been up to the shock of going there ourselves, should we have had the opportunity.

The first significant lesson when company came was that we studied our own community. We can live in a place all our lives and never really appreciate it or even sally out to see it until company comes. Near our native home is the site of a great historic battlefield which is in all the American history books. This is the battlefield where Custer took on the Cheyennes a few months before he made his way up to Little Big Horn. Although Black Kettle is not as famous as Little Big Horn, there is one major difference. Custer won at Black Kettle.

When I was young, we would travel out to the famous battlefield site regularly, once every two years when the cousins came to visit. As we delivered our version of the guided tour, we talked as if we went there about once a week, never mentioning that the only time we saw the place was when they were with us.

The second major lesson we learned is that when company came we did not necessarily need luxury accommodations for a good night's sleep. The adults took all the available beds, which left the kids to the delightful enterprise of sleeping on pallets on the floor. Because we never had enough blankets for each of us to have our own individual pallets, we made community pallets big enough to bed down most church choirs. We all would crowd in, some at the head and some at the foot, and would attempt to sleep under those conditions.

There were two natural enemies of sleep. The first and most vicious was ghost stories. As soon as we got nestled in our pallets in the dark and unfamiliar setting, we would begin to tell ghost stories. Actually, the older kids would start it. Being one of the younger set, I would plead with them to stop, but they did not heed my pleas. Well into the night, they would tell the ghost stories, each one scarier than the one before. And when they had finally exhausted their supply, I spent the rest of the night living the stories, seeing ghosts, and being attacked by villains who had broken into our house, not to rob but to terrify me.

The second enemy of sleep was the bathroom calls. One child in one bed has to go to the bathroom at least once a night. That's natural. When you multiply that by about eight children all sleeping in one pallet, that makes for about sixteen bathroom journeys in the space of one short night, particularly when we all spent the evening eating the prize watermelons we had grown just for this occasion.

One thing I have never understood about children is why the child inside the whole blanket configuration has to go to the bathroom the most often. The child sleeping on the edge never has to go. The one in the middle goes six times a night.

Another lesson which came with company was the way some of the old adages were verified. With all that added help at chore time, we found that we could complete our normal routine in less than twice as long as it usually took. I never understood that until I heard someone say, "Too many cooks spoil the soup." My dad had another version. He would say, "One boy is all boy. Two boys is a half a boy, and three boys is no boy at all." Now I understand.

When our cousins came, we learned that the laws are not suspended, just because a whole group happens to be involved in unacceptable conduct.

As typical farm children, we sometimes staged rodeos. We would go out in the back pasture and ride the calves. This was not on the list of parent-approved activities. It wasn't that our parents were worried that we would get hurt; they were concerned about the damage we would do to the calves.

The cousins, who were mostly city kids anyhow, were fascinated with the possibility of riding one of our "wild" animals. You must remember that in those days, none of us had ever even seen a roller coaster, much less ridden one, but we weren't immune to whatever compulsion it is that drives children to such danger and jolting. Riding calves seemed to be a suitable substitute, even though we knew better. Cousins of any kind are persuasive, but city cousins from California have powers far superior to any automobile salesperson I have ever seen, and we always let them talk us into having a small rodeo.

"Your parents will never find out," our cousins said, but they lied. Our parents would always find out, and at that point we would all, natives and visitors alike, learn an important rule: You can't break the rules just because you have company.

Finally, it would be time for our cousins to go home and our lives would return to normal. But normal after company had come was never quite like normal before. In the process of the visit, we had changed—had grown a bit wiser and a bit more mature. It was good to be back in our own beds, but we still looked forward to the time when we could sleep on the pallets again and tell ghost stories through half the night.

Travel is indeed broadening; but when company came, we learned that people are also part of our education.

CHAPTER EIGHTEEN

Family Travel

THROUGH THE YEARS, the ritual of family travel has not changed all that much. The rules and the equipment are different, but the foundational premises, purposes, and practices are about what they were when Henry Ford painted all cars black. We still go on two kinds of trips — those where we are in a hurry, such as to a funeral, and those where we aren't in a hurry, such as a Sunday drive or a real vacation. We still reserve car time for the fiercest of family feuds where moms futilely try to distract us by luring us into silly little games. And dads still won't ask for directions even after we have been hopelessly lost and have wandered aimlessly for the past two hours. The cars might have changed, but the creed is the same.

Packing has changed. When we were children, we had to pack the car a bit more judiciously because we had to work around the spare tire. In those days, the spare tire was a massive piece of rubber and steel which took up more than half the available storage space. It didn't even resemble those anemic little things we now call spare tires. And the spare tire had to be available, because no matter where we went or how long the trip was, we would have at least one flat. It was the rule of the road.

In those days, we measured the trip by distance rather than time. "How far away does your sister live?" Bus, the filling station man, would ask my dad.

The proper answer was not, "About three hours." Nobody in his right mind would put that measurement to the question. The question was about distance, space across the universe. It had nothing to do with clocks. "About one hundred twenty miles," my dad would say, and if Bus wanted any time lapse to that, he could figure it for himself.

Keep in mind that this distance was on the scenic route, because that was the only route there was. There just weren't as many lines on the road map as there are nowadays.

Part of the traveling ritual was the universal seating arrangement law. Somewhere in the international code there was written a uniform law specifying which family member sat where. Dad always drove. Mom sat in the front seat beside him, read the road map, refereed the fights in the backseat, watched for signs, and served as fuzzbuster, automatically telling Dad to slow down every time he exceeded the speed she judged was the legal limit for this part of the world.

The oldest boy sat in the backseat behind Dad, the oldest daughter sat directly behind Mom, and any younger children in the family scheme sat on the hump in the middle. That was their punishment for not being the firstborn of the gender, and it was considerable punishment, because the humps were high and the roads were bumpy. As a natural born hump-rider myself, I remember praying that God would let me grow up and never sit in the middle again.

This was the way families rode in the automobile, and any family which didn't ride this way was what we would have called a dysfunctional family. The plan did save a lot of arguments. Even before we even thought about going on a trip, we knew exactly where we were going to ride, so there was no need to take our case to a higher court. And there was also no need to say, "Dibs on the same seat going home," because we were going to sit in the same seat whether we called dibs or not.

In our travel days, we had fast food. We truly had fast food, not like this stuff where you have to pull off the interstate, drive up to that little squeaking box which you can't understand, order Big Macs and fries, and then sit and wait until they box it.

For our first meal out on the road at the beginning of the trip, we ate the lunch Mom had prepared, and the entree was a dish fit for a king—cold fried chicken. To this day, I still love cold fried chicken, but every time I eat it I feel the wanderlust and a strong desire to go somewhere—a residue from the good old days.

If our trip was longer than one meal away, our second fast food meal was the commercial one. We would stop at a little store and buy some bologna and bread. If we were on a leisure trip such as a Sunday drive, we would stop by the side of the road somewhere, sit under a tree and eat our fast food. If we were on a quick trip such as to a funeral, we would eat our fast food in the car while we were still hurrying along.

Eating in the car required another ritualistic observance. Mom had to help drive. She didn't drive; she just had to help. Dad would say to her, "Hold this car on the road while I make me a sandwich." Why he didn't like the sandwich she made I'm not sure, but he had to make his own. And Mom had to sit way over on the right side of the car, reach all the way across with extended arm, and hold the car on path while we whizzed down the road.

In those days, one of the skills that young ladies had to acquire in preparation for marriage was how to steer automobiles while sitting six feet from the cockpit.

After we ate, we found it necessary for another kind of stop. In those days, we bought gas at filling stations, but they did not have rest rooms. They had toilets. There is a big difference between a rest room and a toilet. I bought gas at a grocery store the other day, and I visited the rest room. It came equipped with pretty wallpaper, framed photographs that matched, and a little vase of flowers. The toilet at the filling station didn't have flowers.

Sometimes the toilets were uninviting enough that we decided to go with another plan. Then we would stop by the side of the road. We would just pick some spot where there wasn't a lot of traffic, with trees on both sides, and we would use the outdoor facilities. Again, there was ritual. Females always went to the right. Males always went to the left.

On rare occasions, the trip was so long that we actually

spent the night on the road. We did not stay at a Holiday Inn. We stayed at something called tourist cabins or courts. And that's what they were — little individual cabins all looking exactly alike. But we never rented a tourist cabin sight unseen. The attendant had to show us the place so that we could check out the bed before we confirmed the arrangement.

For us this was family travel. Before you young ones begin to think how droll and antiquated it all is, let me remind you that the emphasis here is on *family* more than on travel. Travel is a valuable part of our education because of where we go, what we see, and the new experiences we have. But family travel is even more educational because of who we are, the rituals we follow together, and what we remember about it fifty years later.

CHAPTER NINETEEN

The Day the Teacher Fell off the Pedestal

WHEN I WAS a schoolboy, great teaching for the year meant caring about students. That hasn't changed much. Great teaching for the day meant showing a film. That has changed. We had not yet been overexposed to the flickering of films flashing across the screen, and we were fascinated by any blinking light. But a film during class was a special treat, regardless of whether it was entertaining or educational. We watched with attentiveness and appreciation.

One day Mrs. Simmons had planned to show a film. I knew that she was planning to show one because she came to me during my study hall period the hour before class and whispered in my ear that she needed the projector.

She asked me to find the projector for two reasons. I was in study hall at the time, which meant that I wasn't doing anything anyway, because it was against the creed of studentship to study in study hall. But she also asked me because I was a problem-solver in those days, and she suspected that I could find the projector.

Working as a sleuth on a trail, I went about finding the needed machine. Finally, Mr. McElmurry, the superintendent, explained that the school projector was locked in the storage closet, but Mr. Coach had the key.

That was both exciting and frightening information. Mr. Coach was not a man; he was the ideal of masculinity. He was the perfect man—tall, handsome, quick-witted. He knew sports, and he even played golf. He dressed in the style of coaches, casual formality that fit all the rules. But more important than this, he was aloof, never really sharing himself with us, and from that distance we worshiped him even more. He really wasn't a model that we aspired to. We would never be so bold as to dream that big. But sometimes in our secret hearts we did try to imagine life way up there where Mr. Coach lived.

It was natural for him to have the key to the storage closet because he was the coach, and most of the stuff in there was for his personal use anyway. Knowing this, I started on my journey to find Mr. Coach and to dare to speak to him about such a common matter as a key. I searched the gym, the dressing room, and I even went to his math classroom, naive enough to think that he might be there during an off period.

Having no luck in my searching and growing more frantic every minute, I consulted every teacher I saw. One suggested that I try the bus barn. The bus barn was a large Quonset which sat at the far end of the school property and was generally off limits to students. I had never been there before, but I was on a special mission, so I decided that I had license. I went to the bus barn.

I walked in the small side door without any fanfare and came face to face with four men, including Mr. Coach, sitting around the potbelly stove, and all smoking cigarettes. Did you get the full impact of that? Mr. Coach was smoking a cigarette! Of course, he was embarrassed and immediately stuck the thing in his pocket as if he didn't want me to see. But I had seen, and I wished I hadn't. I'm not sure I can describe the emotions I felt at the moment. I was embarrassed; I was angry; but the dominant emotion was betrayal. This was Mr. Coach, the ideal. How could he resort to being human?

I realize that smoking a cigarette is not way up on the list of mortal sins demonstrating total decadence of the race. But it was contradictory to what I wanted to see Mr. Coach do. It was contradictory to my image of him, and that is what hurt so badly. How could this person who was above humanness stoop to do something so human?

I often read essays from contemporary worriers who tell us that the problem with young people nowadays is that they have no heroes. There is no one around who models the kind of characteristics which we want our children to have. I agree with that, but I'm not convinced that the absence of heroes is a particularly recent handicap to growing up. I'm not sure that our generation had as big a selection as we sometimes tell ourselves we did.

Now I recognize the folly of my youthful ways. My mistake was expecting my human hero to be more than human. Regardless of how noble and fine our human heroes are, they are nevertheless human and will someday act that way. There is a whole sermon in this point, but I will leave that to the real preachers. We all know the point anyway. But knowing it still doesn't erase the memory of that day, the hurt and disappointment I suffered way back in my youth when I discovered the naked truth that my favorite teacher wasn't THE TEACHER after all, but just another person.

CHAPTER TWENTY

The Cotton Picking Gift

MY DAD WAS the best cotton picker in Custer County. No, that isn't wild-eyed boyish boasting. It is a statement of verifiable, objective reality. During more than twenty years of hanging around the cotton fields, I had an opportunity to see all the good ones, those who picked 1,000 to 1,200 pounds per day. But while those good ones were getting that much cotton, my dad was getting 1,300 to 1,400 pounds per day. He was, without question, the best.

Everybody else knew it too. Often my boyhood travels would take me out among strangers—the old men playing dominoes down at the firehouse, the chatterers and gossipers sitting on the pop cases at the filling station, and they would be deep in conversation about the problems of the world, and solutions that lesser statesmen such as Roosevelt or Churchill couldn't identify.

These strangers would look at me, a boy in their midst, as if I were an invader from outer space, and someone among them would ask my name. I would say my first name, middle name, and last name just as my mother had given them to me. Then one of those strangers would offer further identification for all the rest of the group to hear and appreciate. "Oh, you're Claude Schimmels' boy. He's the best cotton picker in this county." All the others would nod agreement, and from then on I had identity and substance in that group.

In fact, it is still my claim to fame in that part of the world. To this day, I'm known as the son of the best cotton picker in Custer County.

When my dad and I walked down the street, I always noticed that he walked with a kind of dignity indicative of a person of his high office. Because I was his son, I walked with that kind of dignity too. He knew that he was the best cotton picker in the county, and I was his son. I was proud of him and proud to be seen with him. He was truly gifted.

I suppose I could wish that he had other gifts — that he had the gift to make bushels of money which he could leave me, or that he had the gift of leadership so that he could have been the head of some small empire, or that he even had the gift of community service so that he could have been the most important of all important people, the county commissioner. But my dad didn't have any of those gifts. Instead, he had the gift of picking cotton.

But my dad had another gift — the gift of bringing dignity to his gift. He didn't waste his life wishing that he were something or somebody else. He just took his gift of picking cotton and worked at being the best at it. That in itself is a noble gift.

One time God wanted His children to leave Egypt and go up to the Promised Land. For that little trip, God needed a leader, a strong leader who would obey Him, make decisions, and inspire the people. God chose Moses because He had given Moses those very exact gifts.

But Moses wasn't exactly the golden-throated Chuck Swindoll of the tribe, so God needed a speaker, someone who could capture the attention of the people and deliver God's message to them. For that God chose Aaron because He had given those exact gifts to him.

While they were out in the wilderness and spending forty years in an activity that one Roman historian called "advancing at random," God decided that He wanted His children to build a tabernacle so that they could worship Him and give Him glory for what He had done. For all their special gifts and talents, Moses and Aaron couldn't turn a tap or drive a nail or sand a board. When it came time to build the tabernacle, they were almost worthless.

At that point, God needed somebody who had the gift of sanding boards and beating nice designs on metal. He had given those gifts to a couple of guys named Bezalel and Oholiab. These two fellows had the gift of bringing dignity to their gifts, so they went to work and built the tabernacle so that Moses and Aaron could celebrate God's goodness.

When God made my dad, He must have needed cotton pickers because that is the gift God gave him.

There are so many lessons in this that I am almost afraid to enumerate them, for fear that I will miss some. I'm also afraid that by making a list I won't bring the dignity to these lessons that they merit. But let's try anyway.

The first lesson is obvious. God needs us all. That's why He gave all of us our different gifts. Somewhere in this wonderful world that God has made for us to enjoy, He needs our gifts. We know that. We've heard speeches and sermons all our lives making that point. But it is good sometimes just to see it fleshed out in real-life examples.

The guys who run the sound system at our little country church are not only good at doing it. They are the best I've ever seen, and because of them, we all have a more meaningful worship experience every week.

The lady who cleans our classroom building at the college where I teach is not just a good cleaning lady. She is the best I've ever seen. And every morning when I go to teach, I go with a bit more enthusiasm because I know that the classroom is going to be refreshingly clean.

One time I taught in a small high school where the lunchroom supervisor was the best. My first response was, "Who cares?" We all know that what schools need are good principals and good teachers and good students. If we have these people, then we have good education. But I learned an important lesson at that school. Mrs. Singer was a key, maybe the key, to the good education that went on at that place. Students and teachers alike came to school every day actually looking forward to lunch, and because of it, we all did our work better. Praise God for good lunchroom supervisors and cleaning people and sound engineers and cotton pickers. God needs us all.

That message is obvious enough to accept when we think of ourselves; but when we begin to think in terms of our own children, we begin to complicate the issue. Let's go back to our biblical illustration. Would you rather have your child grow up to be a Moses or Bezalel? Now don't tell me that it doesn't make a difference, before you've thought it through. In school, Moses would have been a good student. Aaron would have been even better. The reason for this is that schools are about words. We write words, think words, and read words. Moses and Aaron were both good with words. On the other hand, Bezalel and Oholiab were gifted with their hands, and schools don't have much place for them. Teachers don't give much positive reinforcement for sanding boards and beating on iron, so those guys would have sat in the back row, tried as hard as they could to have mastered those word lessons, and might have even developed a bad attitude.

Now, I come back to my question. Does it make a difference which gift a child has? Remember that the issue here is how to bring dignity to our gift. The first task is to accept our gift ourselves. The second task is to have some people around us accept it also. Perhaps the real hero in this little story is my grandpa. Apparently he did something right, because my dad accepted his gift.

I think Paul had some of us in mind when he said, "For we are God's workmanship, created in Christ Jesus to do good works, which God prepared in advance for us to do" (Ephesians 2:10).

Another lesson here for us parents is that our children really need to see us in action doing what we do best. I hear preachers warn us about bringing our work home and interrupting our family life, but I am curious about that piece of instruction. Why isn't what we do part of our family life as well?

I respected my dad. I respected him for what he accomplished without an education. I respected him for how he raised a family. But to make this respect complete, I needed to watch him pick cotton.

CHAPTER TWENTY-ONE

Knots

IN OUR FAMILY, Dad taught tying. I have never quite figured out how specific teaching roles are assigned to specific parents. Is there any kind of prior testing? Is this a topic of discussion during premarital counseling? Or is it just a matter of natural flow?

Mom taught manners. Dad taught respect. Mom taught us how to choose a storybook from the library. Dad taught study habits. Mom taught us how to pound beefsteak. Dad taught us how to drive nails. Both gave driving lessons, but most of the supervised trial trips belonged to Mom.

Dad taught tying. The first lesson came rather early in our development when it became absolutely necessary for family happiness for us to learn to tie our shoes. Sensing the urgency of the hour, Dad would take time off from whatever he was doing, for our personal edification and development as a fully functioning human being. He would begin with demonstrations and explanations. Next came the supervised trials with certain required interruptions and corrections. Finally, we were ready for independent practice, and we practiced over and over again with Dad looking on, checking every little movement to make sure we were correct. I liked the independent practice part because when we would get it right, Dad would hug us. It wasn't so much of a major endeavor. He was already hovering over us as it was. But I liked those hugs, so I tried to get it right as often as I could. I have since learned that this is called behavior modification, and Dad was administering the positive reinforcement. At that time, I didn't know the science of learning. I just liked the hugs.

In those days, learning to tie your own shoes was not an exact science, and it came with two hazards. The first hazard was that the shoe would sometimes come untied. I never understood that. You could tie your shoes precisely as your dad had taught you, but for some mysterious reason, perhaps alien forces, one shoe would come untied, and that always happened at the wrong time.

During the recess ballgame, you would finally hit the ball far enough to run to first base where the class bully was playing defense. Class bullies always played first base, except when they were pitchers. In the process of running to first, your shoe would come untied and the bully would offer his sympathy. "Shoe's untied. Shoe's untied. Hey, little baby, your shoe's untied. What, haven't you learned to tie your shoe yet?" Class bullies were always the best shoe tiers in the class.

The other hazard with shoe tying was knots. Again I suspected alien forces. You could tie your shoes just as Dad had taught you, and for some eerie reason, when it came time to take your shoes off that night, the laces would be completely filled with all those unwanted and impossible knots. There were two kinds of knots — those so tight that you couldn't get your shoe off and those where you could. The first kind were the most danger-ous. You had to get the knots out before you could remove the shoe, so that entailed precise and minute surgical hand skills while you were standing on your head. Of course, you were permitted to use one tool — a kitchen fork. Knots became particularly pesty on those days when you had walked through sticker patches.

Learning to tie our shoes at the appropriate time was critical to the development of our creativity and aesthetic sense. After we had mastered the craft of the art, we could then achieve the full distinctives of our personal-ities and creative abilities by lacing our shoes in unusual patterns. Some of the richer kids actually invested money in different kinds of shoelaces — multicolored laces, plaid laces, and even polka-dot laces. We couldn't afford spe-cial laces for special emotions, so we resorted to different patterns. The old folks used the X-pattern, so we depart-ed from that as early as we could. Some children liked the wide-lace-across-the-top pattern. As for me, I liked that pattern where the laces went up each side. Some children who were borderline schizophrenics would change patterns frequently. For me, the shoelace pattern was integral to my personal development, and I changed only with considerable thought and planning.

Our second lesson in tying when Dad again assumed his major professorial role came when we needed to learn to tie a necktie. The age at which we learned to tie a necktie was determined by where we went to church. In those days, churches were divided into two theological camps — those where small boys wore neckties to church and those where they didn't. In the first kind of church, people had to have special clothes for worshiping God. In the second kind, they just wore their school clothes. We went to the second kind of church because we only had school clothes.

Consequently, I didn't learn to tie a necktie until after most of the other boys in my class had mastered it. I could add that I was eager, and eventually the occasion would come that required that I wear a necktie. Dad, underassessing the difficulty of the teaching task which lay ahead of him, would attempt to teach us in the few minutes that we had designated to dress for the occasion. He would begin by standing facing us and instructing. But that didn't work, and he was soon frustrated, so he would just take over the process himself. But he was still facing us while trying to tie our tie. Tying a necktie around someone else's neck while facing that person is a special gift which God has bestowed upon only a select few. No one I know can do it. Frustrated and panicking, Dad would jerk the tie from our necks, put it on his neck, tie it for us, then slip it off his head, put it on us, and pull it tight. This worked all right except that the inside piece which isn't supposed to show was about eight inches longer than the outside piece, so we had to stuff that piece into our shirt and go to the affair with full knowledge that when we got home, we were going to have a serious lesson in necktie tying.

That's how we learned to tie neckties. But buried inside this necktie ordeal is one of the most inspiring messages educators could ever get, and as we know, educators these days need inspiration wherever they can get it.

Our dad taught us one style, one knot — the one he used. That is the only knot we were taught in the formal way. But within weeks after we had mastered that, through trial and error and talks with our pals, we had expanded our repertoire to include at least a half dozen different kinds of knots. Once we had learned the principle, adapting to the variations was simple.

Isn't this encouraging news? Every day we are being bombarded with reports about how rapidly our world is changing. They tell us that within a few years ninety percent of all jobs will be obsolete. What we know today will be worthless. The educational challenge in keeping up with a world in flux is to train young people in such a way that they will manage to adapt and adjust and live their lives in a twenty-first century that doesn't look anything like the twentieth century where we spent our lives.

But I'm not frightened by all that shock reporting. We'll make it. Just for reassurance, walk down the street and see how many men are wearing necktie knots like the ones their fathers taught them. See what I mean? Students can move beyond the knowledge of their teachers. We've been doing it for years. All we need is for Dad to teach us the basic idea.

CHAPTER TWENTY-TWO

Cream Stations

BEFORE WE HAD Visa cards, we had cream stations. For us, cream stations were our credit cards and our automatic cash machines rolled into one.

Cream stations were something of a regional fixture, definitely associated with the small towns that had an agriculture economy. As much as any other factor, they serve as examples of economic reality during the Depression years.

Cream stations were more than businesses. They were a way of life. And I venture to guess that you don't even know what they are. "Cream stations? He must be making this up. Old Cliff's imagination has done got away from him again." But I assure you that cream stations were indeed a reality of my youth; and now, not only have they gone out of business, but they have gone out of our memories. They may as well be dinosaurs, as far as we are concerned, a fictional relic of a distant past.

To live on a farm in the forties meant that you milked cows. Every farm had cows, and every farmer milked cows. Almost everybody had chickens too, but that's another story. This was a part of the farm routine, but it was also a part of the farm economy. The really progressive farmers, those who were serious about milking cows, and those who had electricity, sold milk. Some would carry their whole milk into town to the dairy, but often a truck would come right to the farm and get it.

But in those days, we and millions of other farmers like us did not have the refrigeration necessary to keep milk. Consequently, we were in the cream business. Twice daily when we milked our cows, we took the milk to a machine, appropriately called a separator, and we separated the cream out of the whole fresh milk. We then fed the skimmed milk to the baby calves, and we stored the cream in a cream can until we could go to town to sell it. Even today I see cream cans all decorated, standing in the foyers of fancy homes infected by antique mania, and I wonder if the owners have any dormant emotions connected to the real purpose of those decorator items.

When we went into town we took the can full of cream and sold it at the cream station. On our trips to town, our first stop was always at the cream station, and our fortune there determined our other stops for that particular trip.

The man at the cream station would begin the process by weighing our full can on his big scale with the wide base and then add on weight pieces. Cream station scales were valuable pieces of equipment in those days. Most of us monitored our weight loss and gain on a weekly basis on those scales. At Christmas time we weighed the packages to be mailed so that we could see if we had enough money for postage. In other words, the cream station scales served as the public weighing center.

After the man had weighed our cream, he put a small sample in a test tube and ran a little lab test on it, measuring for butterfat content. When he had finished that and had washed our can, he computed how much money we had coming, and presto, we had buying power. Our buying power for that day was exactly the amount of money the cream station man gave us. No more, no less.

Cream stations were usually located near grocery stores. Sometimes they were even joined to them, and in those situations we didn't even get cash from the cream station man. We just got a voucher which told us how much money we could spend at the grocery store.

Obviously, this was not the total source of farm income. There were other sources when we sold the periodic crops such as wheat or cotton. But the cream money provided the weekly cash flow—food, fuel for the car, a few clothing items, and maybe even a movie ticket. When the cream money was all used up, we just didn't buy. It was as simple as that.

I use the word *simple* on purpose. It was a simple economic system. Credit cards may be convenient, but they aren't simple. Checking accounts may be convenient, but they aren't simple. What could be simpler than to have your cash in hand until it is all gone, and then go home to milk more cows?

I don't mean for this to sound like a treatise on the morality of consumerism and credit, but I do want to make a point. When your wants are controlled by the cash in hand, you seem to control them a bit more carefully.

The thing about the cream station economy was that it wasn't limited to our parents. We children got into it as soon as we were big enough to climb on the scales and weigh ourselves. We knew what was going on. We were a part of it. We saw the cream station man hand the money to our parents. Sometimes our parents would even go to the store and leave us waiting for the money ourselves. We knew about family finances. I remember at least a couple of times when real economic catastrophe struck our family. We would be on our way to town with a full can of cream, hit a bump, upset the can, spill the cream out, turn around and go back home, and eat meagerly that week because there was no money.

We also got involved in the shopping. We knew that we had so much to spend at the store, and so we would keep a running total as Mom picked up things. Some of my special memories of my parents, both Mom and Dad, were those times when we children wanted a little something extra, like a package of nuts, and they would shop more carefully so there would be money left over. Isn't it pleasant to remember the small gestures of love?

I rather like the cream station arrangement. I wonder if we modern parents don't cheat our children out of a vital part of their education by not telling them enough about the family financial picture. Parents sometimes tell me that their children are selfish, wanting everything. But I like to give the children a break. Most of them just need to understand that finances are finite.

I do have an illustration from a different point of view. One time I was principal of a school which received money from the state depending on daily attendance. I told the students and their parents how much state money it cost us for a student to be absent. We set an attendance record that year. It seems to me that this is the same principle as the cream station economy.

CHAPTER TWENTY-THREE

When Daddy Turned the Bicycle Loose

HOCKADAY HARDWARE SOLD more than hardware. In addition to nuts and bolts and boards and nails, they also sold Frankhoma pottery and dainty lace and rope. The rope section was my favorite. They actually hid the rope in spools behind the counter, but they had the ends sticking out rough holes in the showcase so that you could choose the size and twist, and then they would reel it out for you.

One day I was walking by Hockaday Hardware without any thought of needing anything when I spotted it. Right in the middle of the window as a shameless invitation to lust and envy was a red and white bicycle with all the trimmings, large fenders with real mud flaps adorned with a reflector, handlebar grips with little leather straps coming out, and whitewall tires. I knew immediately that I had to own that bicycle.

Convincing the other people who needed to see the urgency of reality as clearly as I did became a major challenge. I had two strategical options. I could use the divide-and-conquer technique — catch them one at a time and start my conversation on the positive, "Momma said that it was all right with her for me to have that bicycle if it was all right with you." That worked on less than life-threatening urgencies, such as sleeping over with a friend. But the bicycle issue was too serious to be treated with any form of trickery.

The second option seemed the more logical. I found my parents sitting in the living room after supper, so I went to them and presented my case. I shall never forget their conversation. Mom was the first one to join the cause. I've found that moms are usually the first to join a child's cause, particularly when it comes to spending money. As she tried to persuade my dad, he asked a leading question. "Do you think the bicycle would improve his behavior any?"

"No," Mom said with a sigh, "but it should distribute it around on a little wider scale." And with that, the deal was sealed.

Dad had to go get the beauty by himself, because there wouldn't have been room for both me and the bicycle in the backseat. In those days bicycles were major chunks of iron and steel, maybe fifty pounds heavier than the frail little things kids ride nowadays.

As I waited out in the yard all morning for Dad to get home, I wondered what could be keeping him so long. I found myself hoping that if he had had a wreck, there wouldn't be any damage to the bike, regardless of any other pain that might be incurred. Finally, after about three generations of morning had passed, Dad came home, and I helped in the unloading process so as not to bruise anything.

It was about that time that I learned a profound lesson which no one had ever explained to me before. Have you ever stopped to realize that riding a bicycle is a learned skill? You don't just hop on one and go pedaling off into happiness in the sunset. You have to master it, and that requires attention, mental skill, and physical dexterity, in at least two of which I am basically deficient.

I went to work learning how to ride a bike. My dad demonstrated for me; he explained a bit; he held it up while I tried it, but nothing worked. I took spill after spill, always cautious to tear my skin instead of the bike's skin, because I knew mine would grow back. For several nights I cried myself to sleep, not because I was skinned and bruised, but because I had become convinced that I would never master the art of riding that beautiful bicycle. I was destined to live an impoverished life.

One evening my dad came home and again urged me out to the road for just one more lesson. That evening something happened. Just like we had done a hundred to a thousand times before, he held the bike by the back fender and ran along as I pedaled. But this time it was different. All of a sudden, he had turned loose, and I was riding on my own. I was actually riding on my own — traveling down the road at a high rate of speed on my bicycle without any form of external support.

I have no idea what it is going to be like in that great moment when we cross over to spend eternity with Jesus; but if there is any earthly metaphor, it will be just like that moment Daddy turned the bike loose.

At this point, I'm hoping you're into this story. I'm hoping it's just like your story, so that you don't have to take my word for the experience of that moment when you are riding all by yourself. That may be one of the most memorable moments in our whole lives.

But that moment is memorable because it is a symbol. It has far deeper meaning and application than dads and bicycles. It is at this very moment that we realize we are better than we ever thought we were. In His wonderful process of creation, God gave us talent and skill and ability. But we don't know it. We just live our lives thinking we can't accomplish anything. Then one day, Daddy turns us loose, and we learn that we can ride a bicycle. One day we hit a note in singing we never thought we could hit. We run farther than we ever thought we could. We run faster than we ever thought we could. We make a speech when we never thought we could. We write a book when we never thought we could.

How awesome for us to understand that the Creator has made us even greater than we have given Him credit for doing.

I think of Peter who had a hard time getting it right. He had to be rebuked and bawled out, and he went to bed at least one night, and probably several others, crying because he couldn't master this business of loving Jesus. But then one day, he stood up in a crowd of about three thousand and turned God's power on them. Don't you imagine that he was a little surprised at Pentecost when he opened his mouth and all those words came out? "Where did they come from?" he probably asked.

But this is a vital part of our education. We learn that God created in us gifts and abilities and talents sometimes even beyond our ability to comprehend. Our education is never complete until we discover those.

As a parent I sometimes worry about this. I know I'm doing the best I can to put things into my children's heads, things like multiplication tables and geography. But am I giving them the opportunity to discover what God can do through them?

My dad turned the bicycle loose, and that is one of the biggest lessons of my life.

CHAPTER TWENTY-FOUR

Education Then and Now

I WAS EDUCATED in a modern, progressive school. I attended one of the original open classroom, nongraded schools in the nation. (Eat your hearts out, school innovators.) In other words, I went to school in a one-room schoolhouse, with grades one through eight being taught by one teacher.

As I remembered it, the room was a large open place. Not too many years ago, I drove by the old vacant building, and it didn't look as big as I had remembered, but I've noticed that age has a way of shrinking things. One end of the room was a raised stage with a blackboard across the front. The library was a metal cabinet full of books, and what exciting books they were! At the back were two cloakrooms, one for the girls and one for the boys. I'm not sure why we couldn't hang our coats together, but there was apparently some good reason for it. The desks lined both sides, and right in the middle was a big potbellied stove fueled by coal. On cold days when we fired the stove as high as we could get it, the metal base turned red, and we always feared an explosion.

On the top of the building was a cupola with a bell. The rope to the bell hung down at the back entrance. Fortunately, Mrs. Foster, the teacher, was much taller than any of the students, and she kept the rope tied high enough that we couldn't reach it.

Our school was unencumbered by such nuisances as running water and electricity. We went to the restroom in the outhouse on the back side of the playground. We pumped our drinking water fresh from the well, which was just outside the front door; and Mrs. Foster kept time with a large black Big Ben clock which sat on her desk. The clock, unfortunately, was within our reach, and on a few occasions some enterprising student set the time up a few minutes in the middle of the afternoon so that four o'clock came earlier to Womble School than it did to other spots in the valley.

Transportation was of the legged variety, and we kept them tied in the barn on the corner of the playground. Our horses not only got us to school and back, but they also provided some of the entertainment and a source for bragging rights settled only by direct competition. In other words, we had horse races during the noon hour.

Mrs. Foster was a large, jolly woman who could make her point calmly. In my four years, I saw her lose her temper only once, and that was when Leroy tripped her during a basketball game. I wish I had been bright enough in those days to study her methods. I would really like to know how she managed to keep all eight grades on task at the same time. I don't recall any lull periods, so apparently she mastered it. I do remember that she was exacting and demanding, using a blend of commands and encouragement to get us to do our best.

I also remember the competition. We spent every Friday afternoon in ciphering matches and spelling bees. Now that's a motivational device for you. I would wake up in the middle of the night thinking that as a second-grader, I was going to have to go to the board in front of the whole school and try to cipher down the best fourth-grader. Just the thought of it drove me to one more run-through of my multiplication tables on my way back to sleep.

Mrs. Foster was not only the teacher, but also the janitor and fix-it person, except for the big jobs. If we had major repairs, the school board would come. I think the requirement for being on the school board was to be a handyman, because that is what they did.

To ease the burden of janitorial duties, Mrs. Foster assigned us chores. My problem was that she assigned the chores by class, and the only classmate I had was Maxine. Maxine was a nice girl and a good friend who gave it her best effort, but I don't remember her being too strong. Some duties such as sweeping and pumping water were bad enough, but coal duty was unbearable and unreasonable. Maxine and I would go out to the bin to fill the bucket. I would propose making two trips. Maxine would convince me that we could get the desired amount in the bucket and make only one trip. Being the gentleman that I am, I agreed. Every time I agreed. You would think that after so many failures and mishaps with that plan I would learn, but I never did. We would start to the schoolhouse carrying the coal bucket between us, straining and lugging with all our might. Then one of us would trip, and the coal bucket would come down on top of us, spilling the coal all over us and blackening our school clothes. To top it off, we would still have to make two trips.

The most prestigious duty, and the one Mrs. Foster saved to be awarded to the student with the best behavior, was to go after the mail. The mailbox was a mile away; so when our turn came, we would go out, get our horse, and ride that two miles round trip. Not a bad break in the middle of the morning when our heads were stuffed with adverbs and proverbs.

I won the behavior lottery rather frequently for a while, and then one day I goofed up, and it wasn't even my fault. I had come to school without a saddle—most of us didn't have saddles—but that was no problem because I was a good bareback rider, and there was a bank at the barn built especially for bareback mounting.

This was a cloudy spring day, and as I rode right up to the mailbox, poised for the big grab, there rang out a loud thunder clap. My horse, not being any smarter than an average hog, assumed that the thunder came from the box. He was so determined in his assumption that he decided it would be foolish to approach that box again.

No amount of coaxing changed his mind. I had to dismount and get the mail. Then I couldn't get back on again, so I had to walk back to school, leading my horse.

Mrs. Foster was not happy about the delay; and although she said she understood, she didn't call my name for mailbox duty nearly as frequently after that.

For recess and P.E., we had limited equipment, but we had space and imagination. During our last year at Womble, we got a basketball; before that we played tag and dare base, which is a complex form of tag requiring speed, daring, and cunning. I was never too good in speed and daring, but I could hold my own in cunning. We also played crack the whip, red rover, and ring-around-the-rosy. Every time I buy a grandchild a new toy, I wonder if my act of indulgence will somehow deprive this one of the sheer recreational joy to be found only in a rousing game of dare base.

For lunches we feasted on homemade biscuits and cured sausage, because we couldn't afford store-bought bread and bologna. But we always ate an orange. That was the one moment of great anticipation for the day—the moment we savored the orange.

Those of us who went to that little school were a motley crew. There were never more than twenty of us, most of us coming off the tenement farms with one pair of shoes and an orange in our sack. With an educational background like that, no one expected much of us, and I'm sure we haven't let anybody down.

Yet, out of that little group have come two missionaries, three ordained ministers, a college president, a distinguished nutritionist, prize-winning farmers, women prominent in state organizations, two published authors, at least seven teachers, and a county sheriff. Not bad for a bunch of ragamuffins who didn't even have a basketball until the last year the school was in operation.

I go into schools now and the difference is so over-
whelming that I don't even talk about it. Who would
believe it anyway? But I do pray that in the midst of our
computer programs and media centers and art teachers
and kindergarten music classes and television piped into
every room, we don't lose sight of one valuable principle.
Good education is today still just about what it was in my
day. It's putting Mrs. Foster in a room full of kids and
giving her the space to get the job done.

CHAPTER TWENTY-FIVE

The Milk Squirt Tournaments

ONE THING I'VE learned from the sports cable channels is that the concept of sport has a very wide definition and application. I see things on those channels which I never knew could be classified in any world, much less the world of sports.

In my youth, games were more sensible and more highly sanctioned by traditional sports circles. For example, we had almost nightly milk squirt tournaments. We didn't waste our time on things like baseball and basketball and tractor pulls. We had milk squirt tournaments.

Since I have already talked about the activity of cow milking, I won't go into too much repetitive detail here. Let me say only that cow milking is an art form, requiring strong hands, dexterity, and an idle brain. At our home, the cows were assigned to specific individuals in the family. Assignments were based on hand size and the corresponding size of the milk spouts attached to that specific cow.

Once we had the cow's head locked in the stockade, and we got our face buried in her flank, we usually sat there pulling and tugging for about fifteen minutes with not a whole lot of immediate mental strain. We could use that time to prepare our lessons, think about our girlfriends, or practice preaching, if we felt that our calling might someday be in the ministry.

But drudgery can be overcome in the world of sport. In fact, that might be a good definition of sports—bringing excitement to drudgery, usually through competition. Now competition in cow milking is hard to implement because you always have to consider the cow. We could race to see who was finished first, but that wouldn't be fair, because some cows gave more milk than others. We could see who got the bucket full first, but that wasn't fair either because some cows gave the milk more easily.

Instead, we developed the highly sophisticated sport of milk squirt tournaments. We would take the milking apparatus, point it in a certain direction, and see how well we could squirt a stream of milk. If you are a neophyte to this and imagine that we made a milky mess all over the barn, there is no need for panic. The cats came and served as catchers. And they were good at it.

In our tournament, we were judged on both accuracy and distance. I was always rather good in accuracy, but my brother was better at distance. As the sportscasters often tell us, it's important to play within your ability.

The problem with milk squirt tournaments was the limited fan appeal—there was absolutely no motivation to turn pro. The only people who knew what we were doing were our parents, and they didn't approve.

But we weren't limited to milk squirt tournaments for sport. We had other games with as highly developed skills and rules, but many of those fell under the classification of individual sport and lacked the thrill of head-to-head competition.

One of those sports was feeding the calves. When a calf was born to a specific cow, he usually entered the world with the rather selfish notion that he was entitled by natural law to his mother's milk. But we didn't think so. We thought he should share the milk with us. So we would lock the calf away from his mom, take her milk, separate the cream out, and give the milk back to the calf. The problem was that the calf didn't think this was a natural process, and he had no idea of how he was supposed to go about drinking that milk out of a bucket. This provided the sporty challenge of feeding the calf. The secret was to stick our hand into the bucket of milk, pull the calf's head in behind it, and then make him think that one of our fingers was his mother's very own feeding equipment. Calves are not that stupid. They knew that even in a bucket of milk, our finger didn't taste anything like their moms' body equipment. That is when the sport began.

Another sporty event of considerable note was feeding the hogs. Feeding hogs requires a combination of cunning and quickness. In the hog pen, we always had two troughs, a big one and a little one. At feeding time, we would sneak into the pen as stealthily as possible and splash a little feed into the little trough. The hogs would all rush there, snorting and pushing like fraternity boys at supper; then we could go over and leisurely dump the rest of the slop into the big trough.

On the old "Tonight" show, Carson and McMahon used to argue about which animal was the smartest. Johnny Carson always voted for the pig and that made me feel good, because I used to outsmart them twice a day. At least I'm smarter than a hog.

You have probably discerned by now that this isn't about sports but about chores. That's where our parents had the advantage over us in this business of childrearing. They had chores for us to do. Of all the blights and traps of modern parenthood, nothing is greater or more damaging than the loss of necessary and productive chores.

There were many lessons in those chores. For one thing, we learned to work and to accept responsibility. But more than that, we learned that we were important. In milking the cows and feeding the calves and hogs, we played a vital role. Our family needed us and our society needed us. We were economic assets, and we knew it.

To be honest with you, I don't need my children financially. I've never needed them. In fact, my children have been economic liabilities from the day they were born. And I communicate that to them. I don't mean to, but I communicate it anyway. "Do you realize how much our insurance has gone up since you've begun to drive?"

People tell me that young people nowadays are lazy, but I don't believe it. They are as energetic as they always were, but they've never gotten the idea that their effort is all that important in the scheme of the world. Without any important and daily chores for them to do, we've failed to communicate to them their worth.

Let's try one example just to prove the point. Suppose you have a teenage girl at your house — the laziest human you have ever seen. If you should ever be so bold as to ask her to take her plate from the table to the sink, you would think that you are a dictator of the worst kind. And heaven forbid that you should ask her to clean her room.

One day the neighbors hire this epitome of apathy and indolence for a baby-sitting job. Two days later they give you the report. "Best little worker we've ever had. She kept the children, washed the dishes, ironed the clothes, cleaned the house, painted the garage, and mowed the lawn." And you stand with your mouth open in disbelief. What happened? Most teenagers aren't lazy. They just need for someone to tell them that work is fun and necessary.

Now that I've pointed out the problem, if I were any kind of help at all, I would offer you solutions. I would tell you how to find a suitable substitute for all those chores we used to do. But I don't know the answer. Don't run out and buy a cow until you investigate the city ordinance. Whatever you do, don't get a hog. But at least be aware of the problem. My fear is not that we give our children too much responsibility. Rather it is that we don't give them enough real responsibility.

Just the fact that I remember the chores and remember them fondly is the point I wish to communicate. I wasn't all that different from children of today. I had energy to burn and a need to feel of value to someone. But my parents had chores to do, and now forty years later, those chores are an integral part of who I am.

CHAPTER TWENTY-SIX

Getting Ready for School

SOME PEOPLE LIKE Christmas best; some people like the Fourth of July; some people like birthdays. I like the first day of school. Maybe that's why I became a teacher. I have started school every year for the last fifty years.

I enjoy every aspect of the preparation, except getting my tonsils out. When I first started to school fifty years ago, that seemed to be a prerequisite. The neighbor down the street would ask, "How old are you anyway?" And when I explained that I was six, he added, "Oh, old enough to start to school this year. Better get those tonsils out before you get too busy." I had no idea why they wouldn't want me in school with my tonsils, but there seemed to be some kind of bias against them.

Other than that, the preparation for school was one of the great festive occasions of the year, complete with rituals and traditions.

We began by buying new clothes. That was one of the best parts. Getting new school clothes was not some incidental affair just thrown into the hopper of other family affairs. This was a red-letter event set aside on the calendar for months in advance. We didn't make all that much external preparation for it, but we did burn inside with anticipation for weeks beforehand.

Getting new school clothes was a whole family affair. Dad took off work, regardless of the emergencies or crises that might be piling up, and we all went to town. We were one of the more fortunate families of that area — we could buy our school clothes at our neighboring town. Some families had to travel miles away into the foreign city.

The day we bought school clothes was the only day we bought clothes; and this day we bought everything we needed for the year, except for jackets and sweaters, because we got those for Christmas. We also got socks and underwear for Christmas, but by that time our fall supply had worn out anyway.

When we were children, we had many ways for marking growth and making progress in the process of life. We were measured twice a year and our heights marked on a doorjamb between the kitchen and the living room. We would wrap a thumb and forefinger around our wrists to see if our hands were expanded. We would stand on our tiptoes in front of Mom and exclaim, "I'm almost as big as you." But one of the surest ways to mark growth, both physical and emotional, was to reach the age when we could pick out our own school clothes. In our family, that happened at third grade. During first and second grade, we bought what our parents told us to buy, but third grade was ours. Our tastes and personalities came to full maturity and we chose our own school clothes. Although this day is not quite up to the moment Daddy turned the bicycle loose, in the realm of significant memories, it is probably in second place.

Nowadays, children choose their school clothes by favorite labels and designs. We had favorite stores. My sister liked the store with all the slow-turning ceiling fans because it was cooler, and she could shop more comfortably when her mind worked better.

I preferred the store where they wouldn't let the clerks make change. I'm not sure why, but this store was equipped with a whole network of lines from a central office upstairs to the little sales stations down on the floor. When we made our purchase, the salesperson would put our money in a little cup attached to the line, pull a rope, and send that little cup zooming up to a lady looking down at us through a window. She would take our money from the cup, make the change, and zoom it back to us. I could tell you that this store had the best clothes in town, the cheapest prices, and the nicest personnel, but that's not why I wanted to shop there. I looked forward to the annual School Clothes Day trip just to see those little cups zooming along those lines.

Buying the clothes was just the beginning. We still had all those days until school actually started to take the clothes out of the drawers, lay them out on the bed, look at them, dream about them, and smell them. That was the best part of all—the smell.

To this day, I believe that the strongest evidence I have that I am a teacher called by God is that I love the smell of new denim. That's why the first day of school is as big a day as Christmas itself. To go to school and sit through the day in the company of all those new clothes was truly an event worth anticipating.

The next event in preparation was to get our supplies. I use the word *get* instead of *buy*. We bought almost everything, including our books, but we couldn't buy the most important item of the school supply portfolio. That was the cigar box. Every child in every school in America had to begin the year with a new cigar box, and we could not buy empty cigar boxes. So we had two choices — buy a full box and get someone to smoke the cigars or know someone who smoked cigars anyway. We were again privileged children because our Uncle Roy smoked cigars and always had boxes for us to start the school year.

Although the day set aside for buying our books was not as dramatic as the day we bought clothes, it was more frantic. We would go to school in the morning, get the list, and then have to shop rapidly that afternoon. Town was abuzz. I wonder if the phenomenon of the day after Thanksgiving being the busiest retail day of the year is a rather new character of American buying habits. It seemed to me that for full volume and rush, the day we bought books was by far the busiest of the year. Even if that isn't true, it is an idea worth pondering a bit, just as a way to evaluate American priorities, then and now.

As we did with our new clothes, we would take our new books home and spend the rest of the evening admiring them. But Mom always gave us instructions. "Now, I don't want to see you working ahead in those new school books until your teacher tells you to."

Through the years, I've tried to determine the category of that statement. Was it just another totally stupid statement which parents sometimes make as a way of fulfilling some silly obligation of parenthood which says that they have to make a certain number of stupid statements? Was it Mom's attempt at reverse psychology, loaded with trickery and subliminal motivations? Or was there a real danger? I still don't know.

But after buying the clothes and the supplies, there was one more chore in preparation for the new school year. That was receiving the parental FINAL WORD. At our house, we got the FINAL WORD from Daddy. The FINAL WORD was a message far too important to issue collectively. He would call us in one by one so that he could establish complete eye contact, make full impression, and acknowledge that the FINAL WORD had been received, comprehended, and registered.

When we entered the inner sanctum of Dad's counsel, he would look us in the eye and say, "Now, don't forget. If you get a spanking down at that school, you're going to get one just like it when you get home." Then and only then were we prepared to go to school.

I always suspected a conspiracy. Somehow parents and teachers had joined forces to work against us children, and we were helplessly caught in the middle of it all. Nevertheless, we did get the clear message that our parents supported our education and deemed it valuable, because they had invested both time and money in all those clothes and books. The mere fact that Dad had taken off work for those shopping days communicated to us that our education was more important than anything else in the lives of our parents. Now in the FINAL WORD they were investing their love and support.

Right now as you are reading this, thousands of experts are staying awake at night studying stacks of papers, trying to figure out what's wrong with American schools. How can we make our children study more, learn more, and stay in school longer? I wonder if they have ever considered studying the educational significance of the day we bought school clothes and the academic value of the day we bought books. And I wonder how many students in our schools have heard the FINAL WORD?

CHAPTER TWENTY-SEVEN

Cologne and New Shirts

IN OUR TOWN, high school graduation was the biggest event of the year. Since very few of us would even dream of going beyond high school, this was the crowning achievement of our lives, and we made the most of it. The neighbors and relatives were happy to join in, and we worked together to cram into the celebration enough excitement and memory to last a lifetime.

Even God participated, by often sending a severe electrical storm with threats of a tornado, just as way of reminding us that human wisdom, for all its joy and worth, still was not the greatest force at work in the world.

We began to make our preparations weeks before. That's when the man came to take our orders for the graduation announcements. The night before he was to show up at school, Mom would sit down with us and we would make a long list of all the aunt and uncle units; all the married cousins; the grandmas; the folks in the neighborhood who had somehow stood out as neighbors, particularly if they had no children of their own;

and all the long-lost friends that our parents once knew but hadn't communicated with for years.

The next day as we seniors stood in line waiting our turn to give the order man the number which represented everybody we or our parents had ever known, some wag, usually the shop teacher, would come by, study the activity for a while, and issue a commentary.

"Well, it seems to me," he would say with a drawl that signified he was on his way to tell a joke which would be funnier to him than to us, "that it would just be cheaper to take out an ad in the newspaper." Every year somebody was obliged to come by and say that, and every year that same person was obligated to laugh as if it were original with him.

After the announcements came back, we had the responsibility of addressing them. In the midst of that assignment, as our hands grew tired and our eyes grew weary from reading all those addresses, we found ourselves saying out loud, "Why do we have to have so many aunts and uncles?" But when the gifts started piling up and we realized the cause-and-effect relationship involved, we started trying to think if there might be somebody we left off the list.

For all of what graduation was, the gifts were the best part. There were two kinds of gifts, cologne and new shirts. The cologne came in quantities large enough to last us through young adulthood, courtship, marriage, and the first two babies. A few people did give books for graduation gifts, but most realized that the true meaning of graduation was that we had reached the terminal point of reading, and we didn't want any more books, at least for now.

We also got new clothes. Most boys in our community got their first real suit at this time, and we bought with wise counsel. We were usually thinking in terms of the lighter, more sporty variety available, but our parents would come along to point out that we would be wearing that suit the rest of our lives to such things as weddings and funerals, and so we needed to choose more appropriate colors and cuts. What our parents never bothered to tell us was that most of us would gain about thirty pounds the first year we were out of high school, and getting back into that suit would become something of a lifelong challenge.

With similar wise counsel, the girls selected their graduation dresses as well, and then on the big night itself, we all put on robes and nothing was left showing except our shoes. The first adult shopping spree in our lives, and then we covered up the evidence with a blue gown.

For the main event, the gym was crammed, aunts and uncles and cousins and neighbors filling every chair. They came to take in the ceremonies and to use up the air. Climate at graduation exercises seems to be controlled by an international principle — the more formal the occasion, the hotter the weather. The evening would always begin cool enough with the thunderstorm, but after the storm passed over, the night would turn hot and humid. Good graduation planners knew that and prepared by making the programs thick enough to be used as fans. Despite all that forethought, someone always ran out of air during the affair and fainted. We found ourselves praying that the person who fainted this year would be someone's aunt and not one of the graduates.

When all the ritual obligations had been fulfilled and we had listened to all the speeches and sung all the required songs, such as "The Star-Spangled Banner" and the "Arapaho Fight Song," it was our time for individual glory and transition. We would walk across the stage, take that little blue folder from Mr. McElmurry, and shake hands with Mr. Reinhart, who served the dual role of being our neighbor and president of the school board.

And at that special moment, we passed out of the world of childhood forever and moved into the exciting world of adulthood with all its thrills and obligations. Perhaps if we had known then what we know now, we would not have been in such a hurry to get there in the first place.

I remember well my own graduation night. I liked the pomp. I liked the formality. I liked the ceremony. I gave a speech, and I liked the attention. When it was all over, people came to take my picture, sometimes by myself and sometimes posing with people like Buford and Bobby and Walter. I liked the exposure.

That night I went home at the summit of my emotional being. This was the best I had ever felt.

I was confident, assured, and pleased with myself. I remember thinking, "This is what life is. I've finally found the true meaning of existence. It is coming to the top and living my life from this perspective."

About six o'clock the next morning, my dad, without showing any respect whatsoever for my educational accomplishments and mastery of life, jarred me out of my sleep and sent me way out to the very back side of our farm where I spent the day working completely alone, digging postholes.

In the last forty-eight years, I've discovered that life is more nearly like digging postholes than going to graduation exercises.

Chapter Twenty-eight

Music and Modern Decadence

WAY BACK IN our day, songs made sense. I don't think that there is any greater example of modern decadence, of the loss of morals, taste, and common sense than what has happened in the music world. Have you tried to listen to this new stuff? It is atrocious. There is no music to it—silly rhythms, screeching tones, howling guitars played at excruciating decibels by half-naked, instrument-bashing maniacs running all over the stage.

The worst part is the words. Garbled utterances sung as if they are coming straight out of a bowl of mush. And when you do finally distinguish a few familiar sounds and figure out what they are singing, you wish you hadn't. How can anybody growing up with this stuff in their ears ever develop any concept of the aesthetic, much less common sense and decency?

In our day, it was different. Our music reflected good taste, and our musicians played their instruments with artistic skill and variety which produced gentle tones, bringing peace and harmony to our souls and meaning to our lives. Music played a role in the psychological health of the young people of the country. We listened to our songs, and we were better people for it, and the country was a better place to live because of the quality of our music.

In those days, the words of our songs were rich, full of meaning and beauty. Actually, our songs were the poetry of our age; even if we couldn't sing very well, we would memorize the words just so that we could have inspirational messages to live by. I can recall facing a difficult situation which required a combination of wisdom and bravery and clear thinking, and singing in my mind the words of some contemporary song which seemed to be written to give me courage at my desperate hours.

Our music wasn't filthy garbage and mumbo jumbo. It was rich, beautiful, and fulfilling. I'm sure that you are going to need some examples of this so that I can make my point with validity, but I do this with a warning. In searching for examples of real quality in music, I'm going to pull out all the stops to give you the best of the era when music itself was the best. But be warned—this is going to be an emotional experience. Do not read this in the presence of people who would laugh at you should you cry. Reader discretion is advised.

I realize that lyrics without the appropriate musical tones sometimes seem a little flat and empty. But I think you will agree that the songs I pick for illustration are so powerful that just the lyrics on the page will be enough for you to get some idea of the full impact of listening joy. First, just consider for a moment the sheer poetic beauty of the following lines:

Splish, splash!
I was taking a bath
Late on a Saturday night.
How did I know there was a party
Going on downstairs?

If you are at all objective, I think that you will have to agree that they just don't write them like they used to. What has happened to good music? What is wrong with this modern civilization that we have lost the true poets in the music world?

The next example is so tender and so poetic that you may suspect that it was written by a Longfellow or a Poe or some other great literary giant. But I assure you that this was indeed a contemporary song in my youth. I grew up listening to this, not just daily, but several times a day. From such ear training, wouldn't it be natural for me to have such a deep appreciation for the beauty of the English language?

She wore an itsy-bitsy, teeny-weeny,
Yellow polka-dot bikini.

I could go on. I have hundreds of such illustrations, and I love to remember them. But out of respect for you and for the emotional upheaval I'm sure you have already been through, I will spare you the rest. I understand about catharsis. One just can't live in that emotional strain for too long a time. But I do think that I included enough songs to make my point. There was never a period in the history of our country when music was more beautiful or more meaningful than when we were in high school.

The problem was that even back then my parents didn't see it. They ridiculed the music, turned the radio off every chance they got, and held their ears when they couldn't escape it.

I don't know what was wrong with them. In some things they seemed to have had a fairly sufficient education which taught them to appreciate the finer things of beauty and truth. I don't know how their musical tastes could have been so corrupted.

After listening to them abuse our music, criticize us for listening, and pronounce our generation to an eternity of perdition just because of the music that formed us, I finally decided to get to the root of the matter. I challenged my mom to tell me of a better song. You will never believe what she offered. She sang for me this biggest mess of gobbledygook you have ever heard. It sounded like this:

Maresedotes, and doeseedotes,
And littlelambsedive,
Kidseletdivetu, woodenshoe?

Then my mom, sensible lady that she was in most things, had the audacity to tell me that was more meaningful and more beautiful than the music of our generation.

I suppose that it's just natural for us to have a generation gap. There have to be some distinguishing characteristics which separate the older generation and the younger. How else could they ever tell us apart? Besides that, how could we tell ourselves that the civilization is progressing? If the next generation looked just like the previous one and had the same tastes, it wouldn't seem that we were going anywhere.

Since a generation gap seems to be a natural phenomenon, it also makes sense that taste in music would be the expression of that gap. After all, by the very definition, music is a language, and it seems right for each generation to have its very own language to express itself in its own peculiar way. Besides that, the language of music provides each generation with a rather harmless device for keeping its own generational secrets — those little pieces of emotion pertinent to a specific moment in time. Since the people of my generation enjoyed the songs I mentioned before, we have our own secrets. The generation before us didn't like them, and it's rather definite that the generation after us didn't have much appreciation for our music either, so all of us my age have our own little secrets.

I also suppose that it's natural for all of us to be shocked by change; so when the music tastes of the next generation differ from ours, the natural response is shock, disbelief, protest, and fear that the world is going to the dogs, with music as the wagon that is going to carry it there.

I don't mean to jest here. I am concerned about present-day music. I think that some of it is vulgar, ugly, and dangerous. As parents we need to be cautious and alert.

But we need to be wise at the same time. I got to thinking the other day about how my grandfather must have felt when my parents were teenagers. Now imagine this just for a moment. If you had no historical background for it and your teenage children came home doing the Charleston or the jitterbug, what would you think? I wonder if Grandpa was as frightened by the new tastes in music as I am?

CHAPTER TWENTY-NINE

Tom Sawyer *and Baby Chickens*

I HAVE A confession to make. I've never read the book *Tom Sawyer*. Before you boo and hiss and go, "Tsk, tsk," and dismiss me as an illiterate fool, let me assure you that this is not a careless oversight. I am, in fact, a big fan of Mark Twain. I think that I have read almost everything Mark Twain ever wrote, including his short stories, essays, and even some poems. When you speak with a Southwestern drawl as I do, you have a certain unwritten obligation to regional law to quote Mark Twain or Will Rogers every day. So almost every day I get in something like, "It takes two people to hurt you — your enemy to criticize you and your friend to get the news to you." "Man is the only animal that blushes, or needs to." Or, "I never met a man I didn't like." I quote these so often that I even forget which one said what.

But I have never read *Tom Sawyer,* and I don't intend to. It was March of my first grade when I made this decision. We had just gone to get little baby chickens. Getting little baby chickens was one of the highlights of the year. We looked forward to it for weeks, and we made preparations. We cleaned out the chicken house. We patched the holes to keep the coyotes out and the baby chicks in. We bought those little watering saucers and the mason jars that fit on top, and we got the seed ready.

But it wasn't preparation that was so exciting. It was anticipation. We knew that getting baby chicks had a long-term goal which was worth waiting for. Some of those chickens, the good ones in the group, would eventually grow up to become the feast of the summer table. Even when the chickens were tiny babies, we watched to see if we could determine which among them would have the larger, deeper red combs, because those were the roosters and the candidates for a summer feast. Of course, our parents were more excited about those with the smaller combs because they would join the egg-laying brigade and actually add money to the family coffers. But these fulfilled really long-term goals and we children couldn't wait that long. So we watched the growth with anticipation of that one day in a not-so-distant future when it would come time for us to grab one of those big comb guys, wring his head off, plunge him into a bucket of scalding water, pluck the feathers away, and hand him over to Mom to be turned into a crisp, golden-brown delicacy that has no peer in any civilization in all the world. Anyone who has never had fresh-killed, fresh-plucked, and fresh-fried chicken has no right to talk of the finer things of life, because that person has never experienced the ultimate benchmark by which all goodness is measured.

In those days, we got our chickens from the hatchery, if we happened to live near a big town or from the post office if the hatchery town was too far away. The chicks came in square cardboard boxes of about twenty-four inches by twenty-four inches and three inches deep, and the boxes had holes in the sides so the chickens could stick their heads out and announce to the world with their cheeping that they were alive and well and ready to feed hungry children everywhere. Oh, this was indeed a grand day for us all!

But during the year of note, catastrophe came. About the second day we had the chickens at home in the chicken house, a blizzard came and the temperature fell drastically. Left in the chicken house, the little baby chicks would surely freeze to death, and there would be no egg money in the distant future. Even worse, there would be no fried chicken in the summer.

So we gathered the baby chickens, some one hundred of them, and carried them to the storm cellar where they would be safe from the blowing snow. The storm cellar was too cold, so we brought in kerosene lanterns to bring the temperature up. This would have been a logical solution for the disaster except for one thing—chickens are not necessarily the brightest of all God's creatures. That may be an understatement. As a species, chickens are downright stupid. I have not acquired my physique of pleasantly plump because of the sin of gluttony. I am this way because of the sin of revenge. In my lifetime, I have known so many stupid chickens personally that I am on a one-man mission in an attempt to get even for all the injustice I have suffered because of them.

When we put the lanterns in the chicken house, the baby chicks clustered around the light and warmth and would have all suffocated. So we children, three of us at the time, had to go to the cellar, sit there, and spend our time keeping those chickens pulled apart.

It would have been a lonely time except for one thing. My mother came down, turned a bucket upside down, sat there in that damp cellar, and by lantern light spent three days reading *Tom Sawyer* to us.

I'm never going to read the book because I'm afraid that the book will never be as rich as my memory of it is. I don't want to destroy that.

In these days, we talk a lot about what we should give our children, so we give them as much as we can. We give them ballet lessons and swimming classes, but do we give them memories? We give them shopping sprees and high-priced sneakers, but do we give them memories? We give them home entertainment centers and video games, but do we give them memories? We give them college educations and head starts into the future, but do we give them memories? We fight for their rights and involve ourselves in worthwhile causes, but do we give them memories?

When I think of who I am fifty years later, of what I value, of my work habits, of my attitudes and convictions, and when I think of all the people and all the events which have contributed to my becoming this way, there is nothing in all that background more significant than the memory of my mom sitting on that bucket reading

Tom Sawyer to us children.

I'm not the only one who feels that way either. Not long ago my older sister retired from a distinguished career as a teacher, having centered her work on young people's reading materials. After her retirement, I casually asked her if she had ever read *Tom Sawyer.* She answered quickly and rather emphatically, "Oh, no. Don't you remember? Mom read it to us when we were kids."

When I tell this story, people always come up and ask, "Did you ever tell your mother how much you appreciate her for reading the book to you?" Well, I hope I have done that. That would be the right thing to do. But on the other hand, my mom didn't read the book to us because she wanted us to appreciate her. She read it to us because that was the right thing to do.

That's what I learned from the baby chickens.

CHAPTER THIRTY

The Great Beatle Infestation

THE GREAT BEATLE infestation took us by surprise. There was absolutely no prior warning—no television specials with charts and maps and computer movements predicting the precise time and extent. No newspaper stories documenting the daily progress of impending doom.

To make matters even worse, Mary and I were out of town when it hit. Away for the weekend, we returned late on Sunday night and went to bed without any knowledge of the misfortune that had befallen our country that evening.

The next morning I awoke and went up to the high school where I was teaching—uninformed, happy, and cheerful. Have you ever noticed how *uninformed* is almost a requirement for happy and cheerful? As I walked into my classroom almost thirty minutes early, I was struck immediately that something was seriously out of place. My classroom was filled with students. Sitting in every available seat and standing in the aisles and around all the edges, they were totally engrossed in deep and painful contortions of yelling and screaming which looked like agonized laughter.

I searched the room for the source of their torment, and then I spotted it. At the front where I usually stood to pronounce to my students the beauty and dignity of British poetry stood four senior boys. These were boys whose distinguishing characteristic was creativity. Although they weren't all that creative in completing assignments, they were indeed creative in the extracurricular activities about the campus which we usually labeled as pranks.

This particular morning, these four boys had gathered mops from the janitor's closet which they had placed at their backs so that the mop heads hung over their own heads covering about one half of their faces. Three of the prankster group were plucking on tennis rackets. The fourth, amid gyrations which bordered on vulgar, was beating on the desk in drumlike fashion with pencils, and together they were screaming at the top of their lungs, "I Wanna Hold Your Hand."

Although I did not know the full extent of what was happening, I did get the immediate impression that civilization as we knew it had just come to an end.

For those who have not yet had a birthday with at least forty candles on the cake, let me explain. In those days, the Ed Sullivan program was the main feature of Sunday night television, and most people watched the program. It wasn't so much that we chose the Ed Sullivan program from forty-two other options. It was just that it was about the only channel we got.

On this particular Sunday night, the Ed Sullivan program featured four young men from England to play and sing a few songs. Since I didn't watch the program, I have no idea how Mr. Sullivan introduced them or how long they played or what the studio response was. But the response around the nation was scary. The country had been infected with a pesty blight that it might never outgrow.

I make no pretentions of understanding this. What was the appeal? Was it their music? Was the music all that creative and unusual to make a nation lose its sense of reason? Was it the appearance? Those four young men did wear the longest hair that we had ever seen on a male animal of any species. (Keep in mind that we were just coming out of the flattop fifties.) Was it the fact that we thought they were a little brash and brazen, and we loved them for their apparent honesty?

Whatever the reason, the nation lost its heart and soul to those four young men. Within days, almost within hours, the Beatle infestation had become ubiquitous. Their names were on our lips, John, Paul, George—honest names, traditional names—and Ringo. What kind of a name is Ringo? That was the name of the black-hat villain in the old westerns. Their names were not only on our lips, but also were written all over every notebook of every schoolgirl in the country. Their cheerful faces with that hideous hair hiding their ears and eyes beamed to us from every conceivable spot. And their music played everywhere. We all, even the more conservative among us, scanned the fan magazines for some tidbit of information about this mysterious group that had taken our nation hostage.

But this essay is not about music. It's about our national conscience. Why did this happen? How is it that some seemingly casual item or personality sweeps us off our feet? How do you explain the hula hoop or pet rocks or Elvis or the Beatles? Were we ready for change and they were just the catalysts that came along at the moment?

Whatever the reason, the Beatle infestation has taught me a couple of lessons. First, such events are really more important in the history of our civilization and culture than we sometimes give them credit for. When you study the history of any country, you learn about what wars were going on and who was the president. If you have any time left over, you might get into a discussion of the activities of the legislative branch, although that's usually reserved for advanced study. But we rarely talk about what lyrics people were singing in their favorite songs or how the young people wore their hair. Yet, those issues are vital to understanding the development of a culture. Try a little experiment. Go up to someone at the mall and say, "I'm conducting a survey. Name the five most important events from the sixties." See if that person even mentions the Beatles. See how quickly we forget.

As I mentioned earlier, I was teaching school at the time, and I am convinced that if we want to study the recent history of education to see how schools have grown into what they are, and how kids have come to be what they are, we must start our study with the coming of the Beatles. I don't know enough about prototypes or about music to know the cause and effect of anything, but I do know that this was the introduction to a rather black period in the history of our schools. It was a period when our young people were all out to shock us, and that they had learned how to do it at a rock concert. Boys and girls dressed exactly alike except when the girls wore skirts so short they eliminated much need for imagination. Everybody stood in front of mirrors for days on end to see who could create the ugliest hairdo. Fortunately, we've grown out of that period; and when we search for a reason, we now have to consider the coming of disco. One day the girls all came to school with ragged jeans and greasy hair, and the next day they came to school washed and scrubbed, wearing tight, stylish jeans, silk blouses, and high-heeled shoes.

These events may seem trivial to the real scholars, but these little changes in culture and taste were major events that influenced the quality of my day-to-day living.

The second lesson we learn from the Beatle infestation is that despite all our good talk about permanence, solidarity, and traditions, culture is really rather fragile after all. There we were basking in a fifties mind-set of apple pie and Mom, and within one night we were plunged up to our necks in a new kind of life and mentality. For me the real surprise with the Beatle mania is how rapidly it swept the country and changed us. I didn't realize things could happen that fast. Since then I've seen other evidence. One night there was a small fire in a small building somewhere in Chicago and eight million people were without telephones for more than a week. A few years ago, some boat captain in an isolated village in Alaska got drunk, and gasoline prices went up all over the nation. How rapidly and without warning little events can rock our world!

Regardless of all the other positive contributions the Beatles may have made to us and our art, the one thing that they have contributed to me is that they turned me into a man of prayer. Every time I think about that morning way back in the early sixties and I remember those screaming kids and the four with the mops hanging over their heads, screeching at the top of their lungs, I'm reminded that there is only one Rock in this world, and I pause and thank Him for being in control.

CHAPTER THIRTY-ONE

The Runaways

ONE WINTER MORNING the year before I started to school, my dad came in and asked if I would like to go with him to feed the cows. That sounded like fun, so I dressed in my warmest clothes, including the mittens connected by a string through the sleeves of my jacket, and went out with my dad to take my place in the world of work.

It was a pleasant morning. The sun was shining brightly, but it was cold and the ground was covered with a blanket of new snow. We harnessed the team, Babe and Blue, and went over the hill with a wagon full of hay. After we had found the cows and unloaded the hay for them, we started home. Then my dad came up with a good idea. "Would you like to drive?" he asked. And I responded in typical manly fashion. I like to drive anything: cars, trucks, golf carts, or donkey carts. I think the attraction must be the power. There is such a sense of power to be in control of something larger than I am, and it's good for my male ego.

I took the lines from my dad, held them looped over

my hands as he showed me, and we plodded back home. I was thrilled. I was in control. I was driving. But the plodding bothered me. I decided that while I was in control, we should speed up, so I clucked the horses along and they began to hurry. First they began to trot, and I decided that was a much better pace. We were moving along and we would get home much faster. But Babe and Blue came up with a better idea. They decided that if they would run, we would get home even sooner.

The horses went to work on their plan and began to run. As I remember it, they were running as fast as I have ever seen horses run, but that observation might have a slight exaggeration factor built in. But they did run. The wagon bounced from mound to mound. As the prairie dog holes whizzed by, I concluded that we were in a dangerous situation, and I started to try my best to slow down this runaway team. I pulled and tugged on the lines until my hands cramped. I cried and pleaded, but nothing worked. Old Babe and Blue just kept running.

I glanced over at my dad, and he was just sitting there, looking out across the pasture and watching the world go by. By now, I was frantic. My hands were cut from the lines, the tears streaming down my face were almost frozen from the winter cold, and stuff was running out my nose. And my dad was just sitting there watching the world go by.

Finally, in utter desperation, I turned to him and said as calmly as I could, "Here, Daddy, I don't want to drive anymore."

Now that I'm older and people call me Grandpa, I

reenact that scene at least once a day. Regardless of who we are, how old we are, how wise or how powerful we are, there is always that moment when our only response is to turn to our Father and say, "Here, I don't want to drive anymore."

CHAPTER THIRTY-TWO

The Day We Broke the Rules

IT HAD BEEN a good autumn. We had had rain, and the wheat farmers were happy with the growth. The football team had won some games. The high school fall musical had been a big success. And we were just getting ready to think about Christmas.

The only glitch was that the superintendent of schools had called a meeting to try to explain some new Supreme Court ruling about when we could pray and when we couldn't, but it was all so confusing that we weren't all that sure what it meant.

To celebrate our success and subsequent good feelings, several of my fellow teachers decided to treat us one Friday in late November to a lunch out; so we went to Pop's Ham Shack and had fried chicken and beans, fellowship and laughter. And why shouldn't we be laughing? We were young professionals with our lives and careers ahead of us in this land of never-ending promise.

We returned to school somewhat in a hurry, afraid that we might be tardy for the beginning of the afternoon class. As we drove into the parking lot, we immediately sensed that something was amiss. Several students came running out to the car to greet us. That in itself was not unusual. After all, we were the popular young professionals whom the students often ran after. But this time it was different. They had a look on their faces that I had never seen before and have never seen since. Although it is difficult to describe, I will attempt it by saying that it was a look of injury and terror. In subdued, almost calm tones, they told us the news. The President had been killed.

More gifted writers than I have written volumes on this event in our history. Far be it from me to presume to add anything, not a new word or a new thought or a new angle. But since this is a book about the lessons from remembering, let me offer this as a means of priming your memory one more time. The lesson here is that we *must* remember. The college students I teach don't remember because they weren't born yet. My own children don't remember because they were only babies. So you and I, those of us who recall the exact spot and the exact moment when we heard the news, must remember for all those who don't. And we must continue to make meaning from our memories, lest we all suffered that one long weekend in vain.

This memory is about more than the death of a popular young President, tragic as that is.

For me, this memory is about the death of an era, the death of the age of innocence, and that is the tragedy. There I was in the midst of twentysomething. I woke up one morning a romantic, a product of the rather serene fifties; and I went to bed that night a realist, entering the sixties with a full range of doubts and fears I had never known before. That day, we of my generation tasted the real world for the first time, and we got a mouthful of bitterness and deceit instead of the straightforward sweetness we had been led to expect.

I must confess that this memory is pervasive and strong, and it would be oppressive except for the memory that follows hard on its heels.

That afternoon, when we had recovered from the shock of the news, we gathered the teachers and the students, and we spent the afternoon praying. We prayed in concert, we prayed in small groups, and we prayed in the solitude of our aloneness. But we prayed through the afternoon.

We didn't pray because we wanted to defy the new court ruling. We prayed because it was the only response we knew. We prayed because it was appropriate. We prayed because that's the kind of people we are and the kind of nation in which we live, then and now.

At that moment we didn't bother to fuss with each other about whether we should have a prayer before a football game or whether we should pray in the locker rooms or even at graduation in May. We prayed because we needed God's help.

That next Sunday evening as the Dallas Police Station was writing its own version of "A Comedy of Errors," the nation's churches were filled to capacity. For many churches throughout the country, it was the biggest attendance on record. People came to worship because it was the only thing they knew to do. In their feelings of despair and helplessness, they came. Many of them probably didn't know for sure what they were looking for, but they came searching anyway. As a nation, we may not always believe in God, but we do want Him to be in control.

That's the memory that rises up to do battle with that other one of terror and mourning—the memory of a nation coming to its knees before an all-knowing God.

I pray that this is the memory that compels me every time I write a line, every time I address a crowd, every time I share a friendly word with a stranger. I don't know whether this person knows how to pray. That's not for me to judge. But if he doesn't know how to pray, I should assume that he wants to; and since I know how to pray, I should teach him. That's what I learned that Friday afternoon in November of 1963.

CHAPTER THIRTY-THREE

Sparrows

AFTER HAVING READ at least a dozen books during my lifetime, I've come to the conclusion that in every book there is always one special section that has been included just to indulge the author. This is mine. I know that this is another farm story and you have had about all the farm stories you can take. But, as I said before, the message here is universal even if the setting isn't. I do hope that somewhere in your background you have a scene similar enough to get emotionally involved in the tale.

On our farm, we had two fuel tanks—the near tank and the far tank. We used the near tank to fill our tractors most of the time, because it was convenient. We could drive right up, fill the tractor, and be back in the field almost before the engine cooled. But the far tank was out of the way, requiring a turnabout and some maneuvers. We used it only when the near tank was about to go empty, or when we had created too many ruts and wanted to give the ground a rest.

One summer, right during our busiest season when we were working the young crops and harvesting the wheat, a mother sparrow came to the near tank, worked herself into the mechanism, built a nest and laid two eggs which eventually hatched out into two little helpless baby sparrows that had to be fed and tended.

My dad came out in the midst of all our busyness, inspected nature at work, and ordered that during the process of motherhood, we would use the far tank. As golden grain stood in the field begging to be harvested, and as the hay lay in the field waiting to be baled while the sun shone, we took the time to make the turnabout and maneuvers to get to the far tank, and we did that for almost a month.

I was upset about it. Why should we have to take all those extra efforts and go out of our way, just because of one mother sparrow and her two ugly babies? God knew that we had enough of them as it was. But perhaps that's the difference between youth and maturity. Perhaps my dad knew something that only maturity knows.

Life is more urgent than time. Isn't that what Jesus tried to teach us?

My dad has been gone for a long time now, but I would hope that the lessons he lived for live on, perhaps in some small part, in every action I take and every thought which flits through my mind. I must admit that I'm not through learning yet, but I'm still working on it.

Every night just before I doze off to close another day, I ask the big question. I used to ask, "Have I used my time wisely?" But recently I've begun to ask, "Have I served God well?"

The good old days are the very best teachers.